STRATEGIES
FOR
CONFRONTING
FeAR

OTHER BOOKS BY ANTHONY LAWRENCE

Dreaming in Stone
Angus & Robertson, 1989

Three Days out of Tidal Town
Hale & Iremonger, 1992

The Darkwood Aquarium
Penguin, 1993

Cold Wires of Rain
Penguin, 1995

The Viewfinder
University of Queensland Press, 1996

New and Selected Poems
University of Queensland Press, 1998

In the Half Light (novel)
Picador, 2000

Skinned by Light: Poems 1989-2002
University of Queensland Press, 2002

The Sleep of a Learning Man
Giramondo Publishing, 2004

ANTHONY LAWRENCE
STRATEGIES FOR CONFRONTING FEAR

NEW & SELECTED POEMS

2006

Published by Arc Publications
Nanholme Mill, Shaw Wood Road
Todmorden, Lancs OL14 6DA, UK
www.arcpublications.co.uk

Copyright © Anthony Lawrence 2006

Design by Tony Ward
Cover design by Tony Ward

Printed at Biddles Ltd
King's Lynn, Norfolk

ISBN-13: 987 1900072 49 6
ISBN-10: 1 900072 49 1

ACKNOWLEDGEMENTS
Poems in this book have appeared in:
*The Australian, Australian Book Review,
Australian Literary Studies, Famous Reporter,
Green Mountains Review, Island, Meanjin, Overland,
River City, Southerly,* and *Sydney Morning Herald,*
and a selection have been broadcast on
ABC Radio National's *Poetica.*

This edition has been selected from *New and Selected Poems*
(University of Queensland Press, 1998) and from new poems,
some of which have subsequently been published in
The Sleep of a Learning Man (Giramondo Publishing, 2004).

All rights reserved. No part of this book may be
reproduced or duplicated in any form without
prior permission from the publishers.

The publishers acknowledge financial
assistance from Arts Council England, Yorkshire

**Arc Publications International Poets
Series Editor: John Kinsella**

For Ailsa and Alan Meadows

Contents

from DREAMING IN STONE

Robert Penn Warren's book / 11
John Berryman's Death / 12
Wolf, Leopard, Falcon, Fawn / 13
Whistling Fox / 15
Cro-Kill / 16
Fencing / 18

from THREE DAYS OUT OF TIDAL TOWN

The Hart Crane Connection / 21
Blood Oath / 25

from THE DARKWOOD AQUARIUM

Climbing / 59
At the Seminar on Teenage Suicide / 63
The Ratbag Monologues / 65
The Sea-Colour of Their Hunting Eyes / 70
A Most Troublesome Possession / 76
The Mercenary Heart / 79
Tidal Dreaming / 81

from COLD WIRES OF RAIN

Cold Wires of Rain / 85

from THE VIEWFINDER

Rats / 89

from SKINNED BY LIGHT

Strategies for Confronting Fear / 93
Reversals / 95
Thanatos / 99
Skinned by Light / 102

from THE SLEEP OF A LEARNING MAN

Aurora Australis / 107
The Rain / 108
The Sleep of a Learning Man / 110
In Late September the Dunes / 112

NEW POEMS

Fruit / 115
Spring Equinox / 116
The Wandering Albatross / 118
Fly Agaric / 120
Lighthouse / 122
Live Sheep Trade / 123
Hurricane House / 124
What the Executioner Means / 126
The Grave of the Southpaw / 128
Four am, Nuclear Medicine / 130
Scarves / 131
Luge / 132

Biographical note / 135

from
DREAMING IN STONE

Robert Penn Warren's Book

Robert Penn Warren's book
smells like wet diggings.
I open it and slaters spill
like grey water over my hands;
leaves stick to my fingers.

Having been lifted from recent
delvings into the layered past,
the poems are damp and heavy:
here a rotting beam; here a mattress,
its springs exposed;
here a bottle with its trapped marble
like clamorous language
in the throat of all discarded things.

The book is falling apart
in my hands; the pages go to mud.
The contents page has become a stack
of peat bricks, cut from an acre of bog
and left to dry on the Galtee Road.
I put flame to some of them,
and sit back to read in their light
with The Chieftains on the stereo
and whiskey burning my tongue.

I know nothing of Robert Penn Warren –
the poems refuse me his history.
And yet, sometimes I see him climbing
through headland trees, a purple flower
exploding in his hair.
Sometimes I hear him moaning:
Oh warden, keep that morphine moving.
But it's the smell of his work
that keeps me here, fingering through
the poetry of decay; the poetry
of turned earth and all that issues forth
from its black incarnation.

John Berryman's Death

The room is seen through a litre of bourbon:
brown glass distorting light; the crafted
alcoholic stanzas of remorse.

The bridge is seen from a long way off,
its wired arc thrown over the frozen river
where the warehouse lights skate and hover.

He has been here before, watching tugboats
worry tankers into the deep.
As he stands on the railing, his shirt

fills with wind like the sail of a skiff.
Now he is shaking hands with strangers and collapsing
his umbrella. It's time to say goodbye.

He steps out from his life, no theatrical swan-dive
from a railing high above the ice. His days and leap
judged badly, he plants himself in the bank.

Wolf, Leopard,
Falcon, Fawn

For you there is more to the slow liquid dancing of my tongue
than working for sighs at the heart of your loins.

Each time I part the moist petals of the larkspur
and open the folds of the sealed spider orchid,

I drink the silver threads of your waters;
I float my own mouth across your swell.

Your taste is the spittle of timber-wolves,
flecked with the blood of a wounded fawn;

your scent is a black leopard hunting the wind.
When I trace with my lips your flower's vein,

your breath startles in my hair like a small rare bird.
You open and close, hiding and blooming

like a scarlet sea anemone at my touch.
As I kneel before you, speaking in tongues,

my language is thick with the oil of you.
We are sacrificial, we are beautiful, our call

is the call of the Peregrine Falcon, and no matter what happens
from this moment to the next, there will always

be wild animals to which we can compare ourselves:
the wolf that leaves its shadow on the bed;

the leopard whose eyes have been cast in fire;
the sleeping fawn in a thicket of blood ...

And the falcon, riding an intricate wind, has woven
its accurate flight through the dreamscape of our room.

As I lift my head, it circles and screams, its wings fan over us, and as we lose ourselves again

in the salty puzzle of our bodies, we listen, but the wind and the falcon are far beyond our hearing.

Whistling Fox

My father could whistle up a fox
with the bent lid of a jam tin.
Pursing his lips, he would blow the cries
of a wounded hare into cold Glen Innes hills.
Into a giant's marble game of balancing granite;
the wind-peeled stones on the tablelands
of New England; a sound like a child
crying called the fox from its nest of skin and bones.

I was there the day my father blew
the eyes from a small red fox.
He fired, opened the shotgun over his knee,
and handed me two smoking shells.

It had come to us like any whistled dog,
leaving its padmarks in frosty grass.
That day it left its winter coat behind
with blood like rubies sown into the dripping hem.

Cro-Kill

We had this stuff that Wayne found in the shed:
a tin of white powder called CRO-KILL.
It had POISON in big red letters on the label.
Wayne said his dad used it for killing crows.

Pissy Paul the overseer had shot a bullock
and left it out in the horse paddock,
so we went out on our bikes, and the crows
took off as soon as we came through the gate.

The bullock's guts had burst, its intestines
coiling like blue shaving cream into the grass.
The crows had already removed its eyes,
and the blowies were spawning their busy line.

Wayne used his knife to lift the lid off the tin,
then sprinkled some of the powder
into the red cave of the animal's stomach.
Then we rode off and hid behind a wind-break.

Crows are suspicious things, and it took
a long time before they came back.
You can walk out with a rifle over your arm,
and the crows will fly away.

If you walk out with a long stick,
they just throw their black laugh at you.
Anyway, finally one came down: a mean bastard;
a surgeon with a mortician's grin. It settled

on the swollen stomach and lifted out a length of gut.
Then two more decided things were safe.
Then twelve birds were cutting and fighting over the carcass.
We waited. Nothing was happening.

Then one of the crows fell over
and flapped about on its side in the grass.
Soon they were all dancing and jumping around
as if they were drunk.

Two of them managed to get off the ground.
They were like sick black planes, their undercarriages
blown away. They sat down in a nearby tree
and began to cry.

It was terrible. Smoke began pouring
out of their beaks before they fell, their eyes melting,
their wings on fire, and we just stood around
and laughed at the death of crows.

Fencing

High tensile wire, when strained,
is a volatile thing.
I'd been warned how the wire can break,
whipping back through the eyes
of the fence posts, leaving your fingers
flexing at your feet, or worse,
your throat smiling redly from ear to ear.
You hear stories.

I was straining the last section before smoko.
I worked the handle of the strainer back and forth,
daydreaming, watching clouds move in.
Then I heard it: a loud ping like a struck tuning fork.
I leapt away from the fence as the wire
ripped past me – silver, on fire,
with my name cut into its tail.

from
THREE DAYS OUT OF TIDAL TOWN

The Hart Crane Connection

I

There's a connection I've made between
the overcrowded livestock
ships in Fremantle harbour, and Hart
Crane's last voyage.

There are death ships steaming for Bahrain
with five storeys
of corroded sheep yards, the shit spilling
overboard like black hail,

half the bleating cargo either crushed
or starving to death,
and no relief from the septic winds of trade
blowing wavespray through the hold.

Hart Crane rode the full-blown tide cruising
three hundred miles
off Havana, a broken poet at the stern
watching a clipper

pass with a dark consignment
of dying animals: skulls
and sheep skins drying on the mast ropes
like a ghostboat's ensign,

and the deck hands out smoking on the boards.
That Hart Crane
inhaled a line of uncut snow in his cabin
before going over

the stern rail of the Orizaba is incidental.
He was being shipped
to his death for years, and no amount of drugs
could ever change

his destination. He knelt in solemn meditation
like an Islamic butcher
over the wake, the clipper he'd seen now
tacking out of view.

He watched the bottle-nosed dolphins ride
the wash for awhile
and then, with a curse for the halal killing,
bled himself of poetry.

Stoned, and thick with dread at running aground
in America again,
he wept for the religious exploitation of animals,
then delivered himself to them.

II

What is it about a successful poet's early death
that seems to inspire
others to excuse themselves from longevity's
clean-blooded hand?

Mere coincidence that Lowell and Berryman
fashioned their early
work and demise on Crane's brutal years?
A romantic life's

more than burnt-out brilliance surely.
Though after reading
"The Bridge", I had a sense of being
there at its construction.

In a rented room, Crane sat before
a large bay window,
watching two sections of the Brooklyn
bridge rising daily

to meet each other at the centre;
recording the number
of cables and girders being raised into place.
At that stage he had

no idea that the room was the very one
used by the bridge's
architect – a drunk visionary making plans
for an unconnected harbour.

When interrupted with the news,
he opened the window
and for a moment seemed to hesitate
before shouting down

to the workers: "You men down there!
You poets with
manuscripts disguised as construction plans!
Do you understand

the bleak significance of your labours?
You are bolting history
into place, and cannot see the rust beginning
to work its fury!

What use the skills you've inherited when
poetry is ill-
concealed as a cancer in your time?"
The hammering did not cease.

He closed the window and began to write
his epic poem, making
connections between coincidence
and divine intervention;

reality, and what's imagined for the page;
the poet, the architect
and slaughter;
life's construction and its fall.

Blood Oath

It is where sun and world blossom into words
As a tree's lovely frenzies of bloom divide
Winter from winter, month from month of birds:
In such clean space the man and his shadow ride.
See them upon the hills, life-sized and breathing,
Where they will go, how perish – this is nothing.

'The Third Expedition', *Leichhardt in Theatre,*
Francis Webb

I saw stock routes lined with cattle

At school I didn't listen.
Words fell around me: dead words
that I kicked under the table.
All day I looked through windows
at clouds and birds.
One day I looked through photos
in a geography book.
I saw stock routes lined with cattle
and lonely roads in the mountains.
I left the room and walked those roads.
It was great to get out of town.
Sometimes men came by on horses
smiling under their hats.
I drank cold water from a river,
and in the afternoon came back
and sat beside photos
of lonely country roads
with words, not leaves
falling around me,
and a loud bell ending the day.

And you get to ride the horses every day

You can't be yourself at home.
Not really anyway.
Mum and dad are OK,
but you've got to live for them.

I'll go bush. Somewhere far away
where I don't know anyone
and everything will be new.
I knew a bloke who went bush.
He worked on one of them
cattle places. For a while
he was fed up – you know,
the hard yakka and that.
But he said the food was great
and you get to ride the horses every day!
He showed me a copy of *The Land*.
That's where you find the jobs.
There's one that sounds good.
It's in Kimberley, in W.A.
"Transport and house provided.
Excellent conditions." I'm going
to write away and then I'll be off.
You can't be yourself at home.
Gotta live for yourself!

Talk about responsibility

I arrived this morning.
It's incredible country,
lots of low trees and red
sandy soil. And hot!
Might try doing a Harry Butler –
or was it one of them Leyland Brothers?
Fry an egg on a rock.

This bloke called Robbo drove me out
to the main homestead this morning
to meet the boss. He's a bit weird
I reckon. Doesn't say much.
He showed me a map of the place
I'll be working on.
It's called Mitchell Downs

and it's bloody huge!
It's about a hundred k's from here.
The boss says I've got to
look after the place on my own.
Bugger that! I was going to tell him
that I've never worked on a place before,
but he'd probably kick me off before
I had a chance to prove myself.
He says I've got to drive around
and check the artesian bores
and windmills. I've got to check
the fences too.
There's no telephone, but I'll have
a two-way radio, so I can call the boss
each night and let him know what's going on.
Talk about responsibility!
Reckon I'll be able to handle it though.
Have to. There's another young bloke out here
on one of the other places.
Tomorrow night, when I'm settled in,
I'm going to call him on the two-way
and say gidday. Be good to have a mate.
At least I'm not the only one stuck out here.

And the place is mad with blowies

After seeing the place where I'll be living
I'm not so keen anymore. Talk about a dump!
The fibro's got big holes in it,
and the place is mad with blowies.
They stick in the corners of your eyes and mouth.
And there's nowhere to buy food.
The boss gave me a couple of boxes
of tinned stuff, but it's all muck.
Camp pie, tomatoes, asparagus ...
and it has to last all week.
Where's the homemade tucker I was told about?

No use complaining I s'pose. It's just
not what I expected, that's all.
Wonder what that other bloke thinks of the set-up?

I said I'd worked on a farm before

The boss is a bit of a dickhead.
He drove me around this morning in his ute.
He's the kind of bloke that likes
to have a go at everything you do or say.
I told him I could ride a horse, and he said:
*You'll never even get your leg over
the horses out here and even if you could
they'd take the bit and go and you wouldn't
be able to pull them up they'd knock you off
on the first tree they came to.*
I just laughed, but gee it gave me the shits!
I said I'd worked on a farm before,
and he just looked at me as if I'd said
something stupid. Then he started again:
*You haven't worked on a real farm
you're talking about a playground
you bloody jackas are all the same
you come out here and you whinge
and get homesick you've got to be
tough to survive out here this is hard
country this is bloody hard this is.*
I didn't say anymore.
I just sat there while he went on,
slapping the wheel of the ute
and talking about how good he was.
We were driving past a dried-up wadi,
and he pointed to it and said:
*I've lost a lot of jackas in there
they fall in and can't get out
and no-one can hear 'em screaming
I've got a collection of boots and watches*

back at the house and the birds
have carried off most of the bones.

I heard a weird bird calling

My room's OK, I guess.
Bit small and dusty though.
Reminds me of nanna and papa's house –
you know, all dark
with old things everywhere
and that musty smell in the air.
The tin roof is loose and bangs
in the wind, and this afternoon
I heard a weird bird calling.
When I went outside it flew away.
I saw it though. It was small,
with brown and yellow wings.

It's good to write things down

When I got into the ute this morning
I startled a mouse. It ran out
from under the seat and skittered
around on the floor and then
disappeared up under the pedals.
Hope it stays.
I reckon mice are OK really.
I told mum and dad about it
in the letter I'm writing to them.
It's funny what you say sometimes.
I made a promise to myself
that when I came out here I'd keep a diary –
a kind of record of the days and that.
It's good to write things down.
Maybe one day I'll write a book about it.
Reckon I'll call it *Jacka Yakka* ...
nah, that's too daggy.

Helps them grow better lemons or something

I woke up at 4 a.m. and couldn't get back to sleep.
I went outside for a piss.
Mum always told me it was good to piss
under the lemon tree at home.
Helps them grow better lemons or something.
There's no lemon tree here,
just an old bashed-up thing
that creaks all night and drops branches
on the roof. So I pissed on it.

His name is Paul and he feels the same as me

It's so quiet here in the early morning.
I can hear things moving around outside –
maybe it's just possums. And there's some kind
of birds that go tu-tu-tu.
Dad wants me to let him know
about the different birds out here.
He's going to send me his bird book!
He reckons there are wedge-tailed eagles out here
but I haven't seen any yet.
Might see one today though.
I'm going out by myself in the ute
for the first time. Robbo's been driving me
around for the last few days, showing me
how to fix a leaky pipe and how to rewire
and string-up a bit of broken fence.
Robbo's a funny bloke. Talk about swear!

Well, I've filled the ute with petrol,
and there's two water canteens in the back.
For lunch I've got two tins of camp bloody pie
I'm off!
I'm going to follow the map the boss gave me.
It shows the roads and where the artesian bores are.

I called that other bloke on the two-way last night.
His name is Paul, and he feels the same as me.
We talked for a while and had a bit of a laugh.
He's from Sydney. Says he had to get out of it.
Just how I felt. And he's sixteen.
Funny how both of us ended up
way out here. Be good to have a mate.
I'm meeting him at the creek this arvo for a swim.
Says he's going to bring some tinnies along.
This job mightn't be so bad after all.

An eagle-eye view of a white shape

I've made a plan on the map with red pen.
It's my own route, going from bore to bore.
Some of these paddocks have got crazy names:
Greasy Wash, Simon's Run, Hawk's Nest,
(dad'd like that one!)
and the road between the first few bores
is flat and hard and covered
in fine red dust that gets into everything.
Reckon I'll really gun it on that stretch.
You can drive flat out, (Robbo does),
and the only things you have to watch for
are the emus and the roos.
Like to see it from above:
an eagle-eye view of a white shape
speeding along with red dust
spewing up behind the wheels.
I've seen a few snakes too.
Robbo reckons it's bad news
to run over a snake in the ute.
He says they can get caught up
in the gears or something
and whip up into the cabin
and bite you on the donger!
He's a bloody joker, fair dinkum.

We got pissed as farts and mucked around

The ute's a four-wheel drive,
but only two of them are working.
Robbo reckons it's the diff.
There's nowhere I have to go
that needs it though.
And the bloody gears keep jamming.
After I'd checked the windmill
out at Harrow's Lane,
I was driving in loose sand and bang!
I got stuck in first gear.
I know a bit about cars and things
from when I used to help dad
fix the Valiant at home,
and I watched Robbo fix it
the last time it happened.
You have to rattle the gear arms
till they come unstuck,
then tape the connections together.
It lasts for awhile, but
it's a bugger every time it happens.
I told the boss about it,
and he said I had to fix it myself:
Why can't you get your bloody act together fella?
I was late getting to the creek
because of those gears.
I had to lie on my back in the hot sand,
and oil fell into my eyes.
I couldn't see for awhile.
When I got to the creek,
Paul was sitting under a tree
sipping on a tinnie like he was
a king or something.
I felt a bit funny seeing him.
Reckon I might be getting
too used to my own company.
He threw me a beer as I walked over

and started to laugh. I laughed too,
and jeez those beers tasted good!
Never really liked the taste before,
but they were cold and made me feel happy.
Paul only had six cans, but
we got pissed as farts and mucked around
in the water all afternoon.
And bores? What bloody bores?

Says he bashed a young bloke awhile ago

Today me and Paul are driving back
to the main station to pick up our pay.
One hundred dollars for six day's
work is bugger-all I reckon.
The boss says it's good money
considering we get food and board as well.
But that tinned stuff he gives us
wouldn't cost much,
and the house is hardly a mansion.
He's got some pretty weird ideas.
He says he's doing us a favour.
What'd he call it? *A life of discipline.*
Yeah, discipline, as if all there was
to life out here is work and no fun.
Well, that's how it's been
come to think of it.
The other blokes, the blokes
who work on the main station,
they go into the pub on the weekend
but they never ask us – must reckon
we're too boring or young or something.
And I reckon they're all scared of the boss.
At smoko, they sit around
staring into their mugs of tea.
They hardly say anything.
I asked one of them – Henry his name is –

what he thought of the boss.
He just coughed and shuffled his feet
and swished his tea around.
Robbo told me a story about the boss –
says he bashed a young bloke awhile ago.
They were tail-tagging cattle,
and the young bloke wouldn't get in there
among them – you know, around their legs
and in with the shit.
The boss started yelling at him
to get down in there,
but he still wouldn't move, so the boss
picked up a length of fencing wire
and whipped him across the back of the hand
as he was sitting on the fence –
cut his hand real bad.
Then he dragged him off the rail
and punched him in the face and ribs
while he was lying on the ground.
Next day the bloke was gone.
Robbo drove out and found him
walking along the road and brought him back.
He didn't last long though.
Robbo reckons that once the boss
has got it in for you, he's a mean bastard.
The bloke's old man came out
and threatened the boss with legal action,
but he just laughed and told him
to fuck off. One day he's going
to get it I reckon. Hope someone thumps him!

We sat in the water, listening to Elvis Presley

I've cleaned up my room a bit.
I washed the windows and swept the floors
and put a few posters up on the walls.
Elvis is over the table near the window.

Reckon he'd have spewed if he saw this house.
Wonder if he ever worked on a place
before he got rich and everything?
Paul likes Elvis too. I took the cassette player
to the creek the other day. It was great!
We sat in the water, listening to Elvis Presley –
what a joke! I reckon the boss'd kill us
if he found out we nick off like this.

He was smiling and his teeth were red

It's getting real hot now.
I didn't wear my hat the other day,
and when I got home I chucked up everywhere.
Paul says it was sunstroke.
And I had a really weird dream that night.
I was fixing a fence where some cattle
had gone through, and this Aboriginal bloke
walked up to me. I couldn't see a horse
or a car or anything, so he must have come
on foot. It was miles from anywhere.
Anyway, his hands were behind his back,
and he kept staring at me.
His eyes were puffed up and red.
He held out his hands and showed me a skull.
It was white with grass stalks
growing out through the cracks on top.
He put it on the ground
and reached into his pocket.
He lifted out a small black snake
and put it into the skull
through one of the eye holes.
Then he walked around the skull,
kicking dirt over it.
The snake didn't come out,
it just poked its head through
the eye and flicked its tongue.

When I looked up the bloke was
spitting blood everywhere.
He was smiling and his teeth were red.
Then I woke up. It was terrible.
I told Paul about it,
and he reckons I must be going mad.

It looked like the head of a fox

There's an old shed out the back of the house.
Inside there are tins of nails
and bits of leather everywhere.
I was looking around and I found a skull.
I smashed it with my foot
and kicked the pieces into the wall.
It looked like the head of a fox.

A day on the sly, you beaut!

At the store at Ferguson's Creek
they sell everything.
It's a fair drive, but it's worth it.
Robbo drove us out last Sunday.
Showed us a short cut too.
I reckon we could go there anytime
and the boss wouldn't know.
It's good to do the dirty on him.
He's pretty stupid,
doesn't even know when two of his blokes
are pissing off on him.
Better watch it though I s'pose.
Then he'll drive around the bore run
and we won't be there either.
Better be careful.
I asked Paul if he'd like to go,
and he said BLOOD OATH!

(that's his favourite saying).
So tomorrow we're going.
A day on the sly, you beaut!

I reckon it wasn't a fox's skull at all

The people who own the store are great.
They've been out here for twenty years,
and they've seen heaps of things.
His name is Jock. He's from Scotland
and he's still got a really good accent.
Her name is Gwen. She's from England.
Talk about laugh!
When we came into the shop, Gwen said:
"Look out, here's trouble.
As soon as I saw you two boys
I thought to myself
here comes a couple of ratbags."
She made us a cup of tea,
and we ate some of her scones.
They were beautiful.
Paul needed some bullets
for his .22 and some smokes.
I bought a couple of water canteens
and a writing pad. We got some beers too.
Jock told us about some blokes
who came out here last year to work.
They were all young (as you blokes), he said.
They came out here and they hated it.
Jock said the boss hit one of the blokes
because he left a gate open.
Another one got into a fight with the overseer.
They all pissed off a few days later in a truck.
Jock and Gwen saw them go by.
They were waving their hats and swearing.
They'd only been on the station for a week!
Jock reckons the boss is a hard man

who hasn't got time for young blokes at all.
I told them what he'd said to me
as we were driving around in the ute,
and they both shook their heads.
Gwen looked at me real serious and said:
"He'll break you if he can, lovely.
He treats jackaroos like wild cattle.
I've heard some terrible things about him.
Keep your noses clean and don't push your luck.
If you need anything, you know where we are."
We had a few beers on the way back
and didn't talk about the boss at all.
I know we both thought about him though.
I reckon it wasn't a fox's skull at all.
It was his.

It's a proud-looking bird, with bushy eyebrows and long black claws

Dad's bird book arrived today.
It's called *What Bird is That?* by Neville Cayley,
and there are paintings as well as the writing.
It tells you where the birds live,
what their other names are,
the colour of their eggs,
and where they build their nests.
Now I know why dad loves the wedge-tailed eagle.
It's a proud-looking bird, with bushy eyebrows
and long black claws.
I'm going to take the book with me today
when I go on the bore run
in case I see some interesting birds.
Then I'll look them up. Already,
just around the house this morning,
I reckon I've seen a white-browed babbler!

Outside in the sun, someone was saying it's OK

The boss called me on the two-way tonight.
Says he wants to see me at the main homestead
first thing in the morning. Wonder what he wants?
Maybe he's found out about me and Paul
pissing off on him. I'd better think of something
to say ... um, I was driving in loose dirt
and the gears got stuck again. Bloody hell.
No matter what I say it's gonna sound dumb.
Maybe he just wants a hand around the station.

Well, I was right about the gears.
When I got there, he told me to take the ute
around to the workshop. He was having breakfast,
and just waved me away with his fork
and told me to wait over at the shed.
The shed is a big dark place
filled with car and truck parts.
There's some welding gear there too – bottles,
masks and torches. On the wall there's a photo
of a nude woman with big tits
and thick black hair down there.
I got a stiffy looking at her, and then the boss
came in and asked me what I was staring at.
He told me to drive the ute into the shed
and leave it over the pit.
I felt silly standing there with a lumpy pocket.
Don't think he noticed though.
So I parked the ute, and he told me
he was going to look at the gears himself
since I couldn't fix them.
Useless bloody jackas!
He got some tools and went under the ute.
He kept asking me to hand him tools
from the rack on the wall.
I mustn't have checked the numbers properly,
because he kept yelling at me,

and then I dropped a big spanner on his hand
and he did his brain!
Get the fuck out of it you little bastard!
He thought I did it on purpose.
He climbed out from under the ute
and threw a spanner at me
it hit me in the head
something hot and sticky fell into my eyes
outside in the sun someone was saying it's OK.
I held a hanky to my head
then Robbo's voice beside me,
"You alright mate?" then I was in a car
driving back out to my place.
"You'll be alright in the morning.
Just go to bed now and take it easy."
Thanks for the ride, Robbo.
See you later. Thanks.

And everyone walks around looking sad and finding fault with everything

I'm not bloody getting out of bed today!
I called Paul, and he said
he's coming over for awhile.
When he arrived, he laughed and said
that his sister had cut her head open
on a coat-hanger once.
There was blood everywhere, he reckons,
and they had to hold onto her
until she calmed down a bit.
At least I didn't carry on like that.
I don't need stitches, but I've got a bruise
the size of an egg on my head.
Paul reckons it's a good thing
he bought more bullets for his gun,
cause the next time he sees the boss
he's gonna shoot the bastard's arse off.

Paul's a great bloke.
He's the only one I can talk to really.
Oh, Robbo's a good bloke too,
but I don't see him that much and besides,
I think he's scared of the boss as well.
He told me last week someone
had gone through his drawers.
He reckons it was the boss for sure,
but he can't say anything.
Why is this place so weird?
Everyone's real nervous or angry or both.
Why can't it be a peaceful place? It could be.
It could be like that place I saw
in those photos in class:
clouds and animals and people
working together. The birds don't worry
about things too much do they?
What's wrong with everyone?
It's like one of those fairy tales,
where the wicked witch puts a spell on the town,
and everyone walks around looking sad
and finding fault with everything.

He never shoots birds or animals though

Paul's outside doing some target practice
with his .22. He loves that gun.
Cleans it all the time.
I don't know much about guns,
but I can tell his is a real beauty.
It's made of dark wood with grains
running through it, and the metal
is kind of blue-black and shiny.
He got a scope for his birthday.
His dad sends him shooter's magazines too.
He's always reading them.
He never shoots birds or animals though –

only cans and bottles, stuff like that.
One day we were out at the creek,
and he took a pot shot at a crow
that was flying over (I could tell
that he meant to miss it).
The old black bugger swerved
and racked off into the trees.
Jeez, we laughed!
Paul's a good shot though.
I reckon he thinks he's Clint Eastwood
the way he shoots bottles off the fence.
The bottles are the crooks, he says,
and that old cushion, the one
with its guts falling out,
that cushion is the boss's arse!

Things aren't really that bad, are they?

Paul's gone back to his place.
My head still hurts bad.
It throbs when I walk around.
The boss called and wanted to know
why I wasn't out doing the rounds.
I told him I was feeling crook.
I don't give a shit how you're feeling
if you don't get out on that fucking road
I'll bloody well drag you there!
I was just about to tell him
that I really am feeling shithouse
when he cut me off. You can't argue
with someone like that.
I s'pose I'd better go.
At least I could just drive around a bit,
and if he does come out to the house
he'll think I'm checking the bores.
Maybe he was only bluffing,
but I can't take the chance.

He'd do his block for sure
if I gave him an excuse.

I drove out to Greasy Wash
and parked the ute under a tree.
It's getting real hot now.
The heatwaves are shimmering,
and most days the sky is cloudless.
It must be over the ton
in the middle of the day, I reckon.
I sat under a tree next to the ute
and started a letter to mum and dad.
I can't tell them about what's happening.
They'd only worry, and besides,
things aren't really that bad, are they?
I told them about Jock and Gwen.
I also told them about how to fix jammed gears,
windmill blades, and leaky pipes.

Lucky I had the bird book with me,
because while I was sitting there
this little bird flew up
and sat on the fence. I checked it out,
and I think it was a little grassbird
because it was brown and freckled,
and because they like to hang around
bore drains. I put that in the letter too.

As I was reading, I looked up and saw
a cloud of dust rising up from the road.
When I stood up I went all dizzy
and my eyes were blurry. Then I saw
a white Holden ute coming fast up the road.
I couldn't see who was driving because
the sun kept flashing in the windscreen.
I didn't need to know who it was.

He got out of the car and just stood there

staring at me. He was holding his cattle cane,
then he walked over and whacked the bonnet
of my ute real hard. Then he turned around:
What the fuck do you think you're doing?
Do you think I pay you blokes to come out here
and sit on your arses reading books?
He was trembling and his face was red.
He walked up to me and hit the bird book,
and ripped out a handful of pages.
He threw the book and the pages into the dirt.
Where's that other young smart-arse bastard?
I know what you blokes are up to
don't you worry. I've had my eyes on you.
Where is he? He's probably out sun bloody baking
too isn't he? Come here you little shit!
He poked me hard in the chest with the cane,
I started to walk backwards
and he kept following me, calling me
a good-for-nothing bastard.
It was like he was crazy or something.
I backed into the fence, and he pushed me
harder in the chest. The barbed wire
was sticking into my back.
I started to cry, and he pushed me again
and told me to hit him:
Go on take a swing, but you'd better
make it a good one. If I get up, you're fucked!
He was smiling and pointing to his chin.
Stop crying you make me sick.
I said I couldn't hit him, and he slapped me
in the side of the head, on the ear.
Blood began dripping down my neck.
He was still poking me with his cane,
telling me to hit him.
I wiped my neck and looked over at the ute.
I started to run, but he tripped me
with his cane, and I fell into his shadow.
I couldn't get my breath and my ear was ringing.

*You're a lazy bastard, you can't do a man's job
and as far as I'm concerned you can piss off.*
Then he went over and got into his ute
and said he was going over to Paul's place
to teach that little cunt a lesson too.
Then he drove away. I followed the red cloud
for awhile, then went over and picked up
the bird book and the torn pages
and put them into the ute. I put the letter
I'd been writing into my pocket,
ran to the ute, then drove as fast as I could
back to the house to warn Paul.

I asked him if he wanted to leave

I went straight inside and tried to call him
but he wasn't answering.
My ear had stopped bleeding, but the ringing
was still loud, and my head was throbbing.
The bruise on my forehead had opened up
and I was bleeding all over the place,
so I tied a bit of torn singlet
around my head and tried Paul again.
Still no answer.
Maybe the boss was bullshitting
about going over to his place.
I got a glass of water and went out
onto the verandah and sat there
watching ants move over the wood.
Then I went back inside and sat by the two-way
and called and called and waited for Paul's voice.

He called at five o'clock.
He'd just come in from a long drive
and had found a note on his door:
*I'm coming out to see you tonight –
you and your smart-arse mate.*

I told him what had happened
and he just said "Jesus Christ,
what're we gonna do?"
I asked him if he wanted to leave,
and he said, "Blood Oath! Right now!
Let's get outta this dump!"
I said we'd have to get some things
and enough food to last until we were clear.
We'd been talking about going
to Alice Springs when we left the station.
Paul said he's heard it's a good place.
"Anywhere away from here," he said.
I said I'd go home and pack,
then meet back at his place at seven thirty.
The boss has his dinner then,
and if he was going to come out
he'd wait until after then – maybe eight thirty.
I said I thought the boss
was just trying to scare us, otherwise
why would he leave a note
saying he was coming out? Paul said
he thought the boss had gone
totally around the twist, and that anything
was possible. I said goodbye,
went to my room and packed my things.
Then I put some food into a bag
and ran outside to fill the ute.
I also filled three jerry cans
and put them into the back.
I'd already filled the water canteens,
so I put them in behind the seat.
Then I went back inside and checked
that I'd taken everything I'd need.
On my way out I kicked the front door closed,
and in the yard I picked up a stone
and threw it through the front window.
Then I got into the ute and drove
as fast as I could, in the fading light to Paul's.

Two small white lights in the distance like snake's eyes in a cloud of red dust

When I got there Paul was standing in the yard.
His bags were out on the verandah.
We walked inside and he said he'd made
a pot of camp pie and tomatoes:
"We should have something solid before we go".
It was the most serious I'd ever seen him.
He poured two beers. They tasted good
with the salty meat. We sat there eating
and drinking and talking about what had happened.
Something had gone terribly wrong
and we were being blamed. I said maybe the bush
can make a bloke go really weird after awhile,
the heat and the boredom and that,
but Paul said: "No excuse in the world is going
to save the boss from being a dickhead!"
We talked about the trip. Paul had a map,
so we planned how to get across to Alice.
It was a long drive through hot country,
so we agreed that travelling by night
would be best. We could take it easy during the day.
We had to drive on a narrow road.
It went straight through the desert.
Paul had a few water canteens too,
and he reckoned we'd be able to fill them up
from someone along the way.
He said lots of people drive through the desert.
Jeez it felt good to be getting out of it!
I went outside for a piss.
I was standing in the yard and something
caught my eye. I looked up and saw
two small white lights in the distance
like snake's eyes in a cloud of red dust.

Then trees got in the way and we were out of sight

I yelled to Paul and he ran outside.
We grabbed the bags and the rifle
and threw them into the ute
and took off around the side of the house.
Paul drove like mad through the back gate
then gunned it out along the fence
until we reached the road that led
through the house paddock and out
through the station. It was a clear night
with a moon, so I told Paul to turn
the headlights off until we were clear.
I looked back and the lights were coming
fast up to the house. We went down a hill,
and when we came up the other side
I could see someone running up to the verandah.
Then trees got in the way and we were out of sight,
and "GET STUFFED YOU CRAZY BASTARD!"

It was the best thing I'd seen in ages

It was the boss. It had to be. For sure.
He'd really come for us.
I kept looking back.
Even after we'd been driving
for an hour I kept looking back,
expecting to see his lights
come out of the dark and stare at us.
Paul thumped the wheel and said
that we'd left all our money on the table.
Then he laughed. He said the boss
could use it to buy a new cattle cane,
or maybe he could buy one of those
store dummies, and dress it up
like a jackaroo, and beat the shit out of it.
I laughed too. Jeez, it was good to laugh again.
We did have a bit of money with us –
enough to last until we got to Alice anyway.

We didn't talk anymore for awhile.
I said I'd drive, but Paul was happy
to keep going. So I sat back
and watched the moon through the open window.
It was the best thing I'd seen in ages.

The police would understand

The road was really narrow now,
and the sand was loose,
and the ute kept sliding around.
We stopped for a rest about 3 a.m.
Paul fell asleep, but my mind was racing.
I got out and walked around for awhile,
then sat down and opened the letter
I'd been writing home.
I tried to write some more,
but I couldn't think of anything.
Not yet anyway. All I could think of
was getting to Alice Springs
and phoning everyone, and telling them
that we were OK, I was coming home.
But we'd stolen the bloody ute!
It was the first time I'd thought about it.
And no-one was going to believe us
when we told them what had happened.
And if the police or anyone asked the boss,
he'd just make up some bullshit
about how we were useless jackas.

Paul woke up and I told him
about what I'd been thinking.
At first he just said shit, and then
that it'd be OK.
The police would understand.
I don't think he really believed it though.
I didn't.

I said I wanted to drive.
We took off again,
following the narrow track,
and the ute slipped around in the sand.

The land was flat and you could see for miles

It wasn't really a road anymore,
just a red sandy track,
and the wheels kept spinning around.
If the four-wheel drive had been working,
we'd have really been able to go for it,
but it was like driving in mud.
The ute kept fish-tailing, and once we got stuck
and had to put stones and branches
under the wheels before we could get out.
It was pretty scary.
We drove until the light started to show
on the horizon. It was already getting warm.
The land was flat and you could see for miles –
no big trees, just small scraggly things
and red sand everywhere you looked.
I said maybe we'd better be going back,
but Paul said no way, we have to keep going.
Then we stopped. The wheels were spinning.
I backed up a bit and tried to drive in fast,
but we stopped again, and this time,
when I tried to push it,
the wheels went deep into the sand.
I couldn't even back out.
We got out of the ute.
The sand was up to the top of the tyres.
I looked at Paul. He was staring up the track.
"Someone'll come," he said.

It was like a half-buried animal with sad eyes and a silver smile

By nine o'clock it was like being inside an oven.
We'd been sitting in the shade of the ute, not talking.
Then Paul spoke: "I reckon we should move on a bit on foot.
It can't hurt. We should meet someone before too long.
Sitting here's not going to shift the bloody ute, is it!"
"BLOOD OATH!" I shouted, and Paul laughed.
Then we went to the ute and started to unload the gear.
We strung the water bottles together with our belts
and hung them over our shoulders. We put the food
into our rucksacks. Paul took the rifle out of its case:
"Might come in handy if we see an emu along the way."
I'd left my hat back at Paul's. He said we could take turns
wearing his. I said we should make some kind of sign,
so that if people come looking for us they'd know
where we were. I got the tool box out of the ute
and made a large SOS on the roof with spanners
and other tools. I also used insulation tape
from the glove box. Then we walked off down the track.
It was weird. The heat was making squiggles in the air,
and the stones on the track flashed in our eyes.
I turned around and looked at the ute.
It was like a half-buried animal,
with sad eyes and a silver smile.
I didn't turn around again.

He just said "Elvis Presley", and called me a dickhead for being so obvious

Walking in the desert sand
was like walking over hot coals.
It burnt through the soles of our boots,
and our socks were wet with sweat.
It could've been blood it felt so bad.
We couldn't walk very far for long.
We had to keep stopping for rest and water.
When I breathed in it felt like
my lungs were on fire.

By two o'clock we couldn't walk anymore.
We were buggered. The only shade
was under the small trees,
but they were hopeless. The sun came
straight through them onto our heads.
It was better than walking though.
We ate some camp pie, but it only made us thirsty.
I felt terrible. My head was aching
and my heart was beating fast.
Paul didn't say anything.
His lips were cracked and his eyes were red,
and he was drinking too much water.
We'd played this game at the creek a few times.
You give the other person the initials
of someone famous, and they have to
figure out who it is by asking questions.
You can only answer yes or no.
I leaned over to Paul and said:
"Here's one for you mate ... E.P."
Paul didn't even bother asking any questions.
He just said, "Elvis Presley," and called me
a dickhead for being so obvious.

As if he could see death coming out of the desert

I fell asleep, but kept waking up.
The flies were sticky, and the sun
was stinging my arms and neck.
Paul was lying on his back
with his hat over his face.
I was too buggered to start talking,
but I wanted to see Paul move.
I flicked a stone at him,
and he moaned and lifted his hand
then let it fall back to his chest.
The sun was getting lower,
but it was still like fire in the air.

The shadows of the stones were thick
and blue on the ground.
The heat was hanging over us.
We wouldn't see anyone out here.
The place was empty except for
lizards and birds and trees.
And even they must hate the heat.
And the sun makes you think weird things.
I was real thirsty and I thought of Robbo.
He came walking up the track
with a carton of beers under his arm.
"Hey, Robbo, come over here you lucky bugger
give us a beer will ya the weatherman's voice
on the radio saying tomorrow will be fine
this afternoon's temperature is deadly
this beer is great Robbo crack another one ..."

Paul rolled over and reached for the water bottle.
He unscrewed the top and tipped
the bottle up to his mouth.
It was empty, so he chucked it over his shoulder.
I threw him mine and he took a slug.
"We're ratshit mate," he said.
He was looking past me into the desert.
His eyes looked really strange,
like they were empty or something.
He was staring out into the dust
as if he could see death coming out of the desert.
I closed my eyes and saw it too.
Death was a great black animal
coming silently out of the trees.

Sometime in the night I heard Paul talking

When it got dark it was cooler
and we could move around a bit.
Our faces were bright red, and our lips

were all cracked and blistered.
My head was thick and sore.
Paul said it felt as though
his guts were about to burst.
There was only one water bottle left.
We decided not to drink anymore
before morning, and that we should
get going early, before it got too hot.
I don't know how, but we slept.
Sometime in the night I heard Paul talking.
I couldn't make out everything he said,
but I heard: "Let's go to the creek, mate!"
I whispered that it was a great idea,
and then tried to get some sleep,
and listened to the desert,
and waited for the sun.

He was tired and wanted to lie down for a while

I gave Paul a nudge.
It was still dark,
but there was a pale line of light
stretching out across the horizon.
He told me to piss off,
but I kept at him until he got up.
He looked bad. We put our boots on
and started walking.
We walked for a long time
without saying anything.
Every step felt funny
like walking on cotton wool.
I felt all wobbly in the legs,
and my face was hurting bad.
Paul kept saying that
he couldn't breathe very well.
He kept falling back
and was asking for water:

"Give me the water bottle mate,
the water bottle, shit!"
We stopped and had a drink
and finished the water.
We'd been walking for ages
but hadn't come very far.
Maybe someone flying over
would see the sign on the roof.
Paul stumbled and fell over.
He said he was tired
and wanted to lie down for awhile.
I told him we had to keep going,
but I wanted to lie down too.
"Come on mate, someone'll find us.
Someone'll turn up sooner or later."
Paul just shook his head
and sat down at the side of the track.
"You go on for awhile.
I'll stay here and mind the ute."
I left him there and walked off.
The heat came off the sand
and hit me in the face.
I couldn't see very well.
Every now and then there were tracks
running off to the left and right.
I kept going. Then my legs went numb.
I left the track and fell over.
I crawled under a tree
and propped myself up.
I got the letter out of my pocket
but couldn't read a word.
So I put a stone on it
and closed my eyes.

In a quiet place filled with eagles

The desert started to call out

the heat was blue
and the sky was on fire
behind my eyes the sun exploded
a black lizard walked up and said hello
before it cartwheeled over the sand
the wind was hot and angry
then a big bird sailed over
its shadow gliding over the ground
it wasn't flapping at all
I followed it through the sky
it came back and looked down at me
I wasn't scared
I knew what it was
when it had gone I heard
a loud bang up the track
the bird's wings still
covered the sand
reaching out over the desert
the wingspan of an eagle
my heart was speaking quickly
I lay down beside the lizard
under a tree where the air was blue
and it was quiet where death came
out of the desert like a dog
or a gliding bird
then Paul walked up to me
he looked really good
he told me to let go
it's not so bad he said
so I let go
and we went out together
over the desert
to where eagles gather
and the rain is cool and blue
as sleep and love
in a quiet place filled with eagles.

from
THE DARKWOOD AQUARIUM

Climbing

"After another interminable winter ...
a young man's mind turns to rock."
                    Chris Craggs

THE CHIMES OF FREEDOM

Climbing an unbolted and very blocky corner
of the Chimes of Freedom,
two Welsh ascensionists hang like stalled buzzards,
their ropes trailing blue against black granite.
It's obvious from where I'm standing
that an epic is in progress.
They are into a fissure so wild
it seems no boot or finger could address it,
the clag coming down over the pass
and the wind like a great white wing
clipping the bloodless mantelshelf.
A ragged hole of sky is their only salvation
and that as black as a Lancashire quarry.
One man speaks out from his spidery position,
his voice coming down like shifting scree.
They are floating on the edge of all things,
the pinnacle of stone they've yet to climb
glinting briefly in a show of Cambrian sun
with all the weight and acuity of a Kilimanjaro icicle.
I expect a Steeleye Span ballad to break through
like the folky soundtrack to a climbing documentary,
but wind and shouts of encouragement
are all I can discern from the sheer
undrilled acoustics of the wall.
Later, they'll either be holed up
in the climber-crowded pub that adjoins the vicarage,
extolling loudly the Chimes of Freedom's virtues
and soaking printless fingertips in spirit;
they'll be up there still, splashing Fairy Liquid
liberally over a jammed and wind-bitten limb;
or they'll be lying where I'm standing,
at the base of dragon-printed rocks,
their ropes curled about them like the tendrils

of alpine flowers. Whatever their situation,
sitting red-faced over a row of pints,
suspended in a windy fitful sleep, or breaking down
to fertilise a barren hill, their expressions
will be set in true descriptions
of what they've just encountered:
wide-eyed, open-mouthed, in any case amazed.

The Nameless Tower of Trango

throws a late afternoon shadow
like the deep body-print of a fallen giant.
If you believe half the climbers
that worship at the lofty altars
these crags provide, then giants exist,
their great palms extended
under difficult ascensions
like safety nets for surrealist adventurers.
The other half, while celebrating
the magical qualities of each climb,
refuse to entertain celestial myth and legend –
no wings or hands of guidance
bearing them aloft, no rope-fraying demons,
just hard slog on geography
most people see as nesting sites for falcons,
suicide launching pads.

Who gives these walls of stone their names?
Free-climbing poets in mountain drag no doubt,
the shape of their hands
stencilled whitely onto rock
as they mark their passage with chalk
on a face of original granite.
Maybe one of them thought of the name as she climbed,
lifting it as Tolkien did
from the rings of pipesmoke he fired
across the room – though her smoke

was the dust her fingers disturbed
from a chalk bag worn like a velvet bladder
dispensing runes: an upside-down thumbprint
a symbol for danger on a fracture line,
a two-fingered powdersmear an emblem for safety
as she paused for breath and surveillance.
Though most likely she chose the name
collapsed on a litter of birdshit
and camming devices, her pulse
like the motor of a labouring inclinator.
And because she was one who understood
that all things can be made amazing
by a balanced imagination, lights
in the valley like miner's lanterns
emerging from the gloom and the darkening
wall of stone she'd claimed as her own
became the Nameless Tower of Trango,
protected by gryphons and the rain-blurred
spectres of Celtic fell walkers, throwing a shadow
like the deep body-print of a fallen giant
she wanted desperately to believe in.

The Abyss

Terror has nailed the best of them to the rock
at least once in a climbing life,
and not always on the first attempt.
Many have seen a great view go to buggery
as they palpitated like moths
pinned to a textured card.
                    Fear is the body's
camouflage, changing flesh to match the colour
of the stone they're on, so that Death,
who loves a risk, won't notice them
as it eases itself up the same fingerholds
like a sloth with crampons fixed to its paws.
Mostly Death passes over them, raking their backs

and mistaking tangled ropes for fibrous roots
tracking the crag for sustenance. Though sometimes,
the rope worn through or the bolt flying free,
Death takes them in the fireman's carry
like an abseiling undertaker into the abyss.

At the Seminar on Teenage Suicide

I turn away from the overhead projector's
small white box with its bar graph
of black columns stacked like upended
coffins for children of various sizes.
The window is filled with rain –
feather-shaped streams washing the glass,
and trees in the yard look like
they're melting. I open the window.
Three crows are inspecting the contents
of an overturned rubbish bin. Behind me,
the counsellor's words are thick
with images of death. I catch fragments
of his talk as the crows scatter paper
like clothes at a rummage sale:
Depression manifests itself ... One crow
rakes another with its feet. *Carbon
monoxide* ... I see four young people
in a car on a country road. They are
locked arm in arm, the windows wound up
and fogged with blue smoke as they
swallow their exhaustion.
                        Now the rain
is a tiled whisper on the library roof.
A whisper, like someone planning to resolve
the problem their life has become.
To hear the details of how these children
take their lives removes me to an afternoon
on Town Hall Station. Underground, and numb
with resignation, I watched the spaces
between the carriages and the line – a dark
place, where rats hurry over the sleepers
when the trains are still. I was waiting
for the urge to die to carry me away.
I counted fifteen trains, and when I did
rise to go, I went back home, crying over
the harbour, leaving my death
to blow away in the wake of passing trains.

And now the lights go out. A power failure
disconnects the projector's sad statistics
from the screen. In the dark we do not move,
and our talk concerns the storm. I imagine
the shapes of children emerging from under
the trees. Their bodies are transparent now
that living is a burden, dying a release.
How desperately they want us to listen
to their stories! Some have crows flapping
darkly behind their eyes, their pockets over-
spilling with death's inventions. Others
remain in the distance, marking time where
indecision draws and then repels them from
the prospect of their end. I climb through
the window and go to them. We sit in the rain,
exchanging reasons: the pressures of exams,
the fast world's lists of expectations and
demands. They take comfort when I tell them
that I too have explored the edge; that life
excused me briefly once, then returned me
when I felt my heart move like a small animal
inside my shirt. As we talk, their bodies
begin to repair themselves. They empty into
the grass capsules and bottles of over-
proof escape.
         The rain stops,
a crow calls in the distance, and the lights
flicker on in the room. Imagination pales
to a row of dripping trees, their branches
closing around the lives of frightened
children, aware now of the urgent pulsing
of their hearts, being careful with themselves.

The Ratbag Monologues

Eternity

For years I wrote *Eternity* in copperplate
on Sydney's streets. There was something calm
about leaving the word chalked onto bitumen.
A friend once said it was like reading
a streetname one encounters in a dream.
Sometimes I'd return to the place, and there
might be someone admiring what I'd done,
though once I overheard a woman say
that whoever wrote it must be gone in the head.
As far as I know, they never rubbed it off.
Eternity lasted a week or two, depending
on the weather – rain and wind made the word
look like pale veins in opened stone.
Then everyone was trying to guess my name.
The press spoke of God, and my belief
in the afterlife, but really, it was nothing
like that. I loved the sound and feel of the word,
the way it floated, the way my hand
moved in shadow as I wrote it down.
Then I stopped writing. It wasn't because
they'd discovered my name, or because I'd grown
tired of writing without a signature.
There was no reason. In the papers they suggested
that I'd died, which disappointed me.
I still went out to the streets alone,
and at the Sydney Town Hall I listened
to the bells, and waited for them to empty
the spires of pigeons. And one night, in my room,
smoking by the window, I blew a perfect ring
and watched as it dispersed
like chalkdust blown from tar.

The Domain

On a box in the Domain, on Sunday afternoons,
if the time and the whiskey were moving me to talk,
then perhaps I'd tell the story of a man
of constant sorrow, whose appointment with grief
left him nailed like a paradise bird to Jerusalem wood;
and how, before he could rise,
he requested water from the garrison, and the flies
laid their eggs like a blessing in his side.
And if a crowd had gathered, I'd take a slug
and ask them to watch the angels passing overhead –
a bright parade, wired into formation
over the harbour, revolving slowly there
like a mobile on strings of salty wind.
And often in the loud stand of common prayer,
the hecklers would project their spit like flak
for sky pilots. They kept me honest as I worked
unlicensed in the trade of spoken love.
From my box I saw the trees and faces blur,
and the houses shouldering each other down the road.
People came to listen, and some to tell
whatever it was they were busting to say.
There was a man who played guitar,
thrashing away until his fingers bled. And Jeanie,
who took her clothes off in the rain, and climbed
the twisted arms of a Moreton Bay fig,
waving her wet black stockings at the sky.
When I was young, from my father's shoulders
the speakers looked like puppets on a box
that dance when you press your thumb.
Then one day I started dancing, working through
stories in the Bible, the language of the prophets
coming to me as poetry: John the Baptist, Amos
and Isaiah, released like children to shout across the park,
and the wind creaming their voices into the trees.

Mary

With Jack gone, I feel like a piece of my side is missing.
One night he turned over from a bad sleep, spoke my name
and died. I walked into town, leaving him wrapped
in his blanket on the bed. The ambulance came out
and took him away. At the funeral I couldn't cry.
I went home, opened a bottle, and drank until the sound
of dirt hitting his coffin disappeared.
The welfare people were kind. They gave me clothes
and food, but they took all the drink we had.
The doctors say I'll die too if I don't stop drinking.
It's hard though. In winter, Jack and I
put our coats on and sat in the bus shelter,
watching the shoppers come and go in their cars.
We had a bottle in each pocket, and sometimes
we'd stay all day, drinking and playing games
with the letters on the numberplates.
I don't go out much now. Yesterday I went to see
Jack's grave. I felt a bit funny sitting there
looking at his name on the stone. I wanted to talk,
but some people were standing near, so I tried
to see his face instead. After I saw him I went home.
It's hard to sleep alone. I drink to keep from being scared.
Jack always held my hand in the dark.

The Fan

Anyway, I'd just opened my oriental fan
with the usual flourish (it's a lovely
broad silk fan from Nara in Japan,
with a pair of hummingbirds and a splash
of white blossom over a bamboo grove),
and I was standing outside Museum Station's
black iron concertina gates, curtseying
to my friends and fanning myself,
when this animal approaches me,
grabs my fan, and shoves me into the wall.
Drunk he was, and dangerous. I could smell
the vomit on his breath. And then
he started punching me. I screamed
to make him stop, but he didn't, he just
laughed and hit me again, and no one
came to help. He left me wired to a bottle
in emergency. Five days I was in there,
and when I came out with red eyes
and a stitched-up lip that looked like
it had a line of ants crawling over it,
I went back to the station
and the news man handed me my fan.
It was torn, and there were blood spots
all over it. They looked quite good though,
just like red blossoms. Then I waved
to all the people, fanned myself,
and went down the steps and waited
for the train to come and take me home,
and no one asked where I'd been or anything.

The Barrow Man

People call me the Barrow Man.
I push my life around in a box.
But no one knows the quiet dark
my sleep involves, though many
have tried to follow me home.
They want to know what's in the box.
They ask me, but I don't reply.
If I told them it contained
the bones of everyone who's ever
asked me what's inside the box,
would they still demand to know?
The Hyde Park gulls and pigeons
have seen where I begin and end
my days, and children, though they
call me "funny man", and ask me
what's inside the box, they know
the secret places I have seen,
and what it's like to live inside
a world that's big and fast. Children
know that dreams are hard to hide.
Sometimes I go down to the Quay
and watch the ferries coming in.
Down beside the knocking wharf,
the crabs move slowly in the dark
like wet black spiders on the wood.
I watch them and I listen
to ferries churning water as they leave.
And always, in the shadows,
there is someone asking me the same
two questions as I rise to go:
"What's it like to live that way?"
"What's inside the box?"

The Sea-Colour of Their Hunting Eyes

I

Anxiety was not to be found
in the violent passage
of a converted crayboat,
though waves were folding
over the deckboards
and the crew were at the rail
all morning, their open mouths
making a sound like wind
in the mast wires.

It was not to be found
in the desperate struggle
of a fish being hauled
hand over fist
from the refuge and beauty
of its spawning ground,
magnified by water
and the angler's imagination.

Nor was it to be found
in the strange geometry
of a snagged anchor,
its chain a rusting garland
around gutted brain-coral
ten fathoms down.

Anxiety was in the shape and voice
of a man in a deckchair
at the water's edge, the cliffs
of an unpeopled island
rising behind him,
the burrowing betongs
nosing through mounds
of seaweed, birdshit and bones.
The man was not alone,
his friends were asleep

on the beach, their faces
glowing in tidewood firelight.
But he was screaming.
A burgundy moon
stained the sand around his feet
like a wash of blood.
He screamed, and the nightbirds
flew low across Hospital Bay,
sipping moonlight from the waves.
A woman moved fitfully
inside her sleeping bag,
dreaming of a man in a deckchair
screaming at the water's edge.

II

He woke to a windswept morning,
smoke from a dying fire
in his eyes, and moonlight
on the face of a sleeping woman.
There was an empty space
on a mattress beside her
where two crays had flicked
their tails and died.
He wanted to move across the sand
and take the woman in his arms,
to smell the sea in her hair,
to say of the night that
it needed love and sanctuary.
But the moment passed.

III

Anxiety had left him.
On the boat, another day
on the make, he watched
the shoreline until he found her.
She was walking slowly along
the crest of a brownstone cliff.
He waved but wasn't sure
if she'd responded with her hand.
He saw a pair of eagles hunched
like children in overcoats.
Later, she told him
that the eagles had free-fallen
from the cliff. He wished
he'd been there, to see the white
feathers on their undersides,
to find a poem in the sea-
colour of their hunting eyes.
But he was offshore, feeding
line to deep blue water, his hook
through the mantle of a cuttlefish.
Once, when he turned
to face the land, he thought
he saw an eagle outlined
against dark stone.
But when it moved, it became
a woman bending
to gather her things from the sand.

IV

Wavespray and the cracking
of a tall white sail, the skipper
asleep in the metal cavity
of a roped-off lifeboat,
the sea coming at them furiously,
the islands diminishing
to a pale brown line.
He sat in a deckchair
and this time he wasn't screaming.
She sat beside him, her face
white as the feathers
of the eagles they'd been watching
though he didn't let on.
They stared at the horizon.
When she went to the railing,
he held her by the belt.
As the boat pitched and rolled
the past came into view.
They spoke of childhood
thrashings, of brothers
and sisters, of parents
whose love involved
gentle breath and pain.
As they passed a scallop boat
anchored whitely to the swell,
he wanted to say that poetry
was a way he'd found
of working through the puzzle
of his days, but she was crying,
her hair across her eyes.
He left her then, thinking
she might need to be alone,
when he should have held her
when he should have
kissed away her tears.

V

At its mooring the boat was still.
The fish were lined up along
the jetty's blood-black boards.
She knelt beside the jewelled
flanks of spangled emperor,
following the blue lines
that sparked from their eyes.

VI

In the car, he sat among a salty
litter of bags and surfboards,
giving directions home.
She sat on his knees
because there was no room
and he held her gently, his hands
on her waist and shoulder.
He thought to trace the shape
of an eagle with his finger on her back,
but he was home, and she was
free-falling away from him.

VII

4 a.m. and a poem is taking shape.
In the shower, he has to lean
against the wall as the bathtub
rolls and hot water floods his face.
He goes into his room, works
on images of eagles stalled
on warm wind above ragged hills;
of two people in a rowdy sea
entertaining the terns
with their swimming's synchronicity.
He parts the curtains and finds
darkness uprooting the seeds of afternoon
like eagle fledglings rising flightless
from an overgrown yard.

A Most Troublesome Possession

One thousand miles, the landscape predictable
and contained as in a sandbox diorama,
the highway's vanishing-point painted
onto cardboard backing, mirage-flooded
at the summit and planted with grey sticks
for poles – the bush telegraph wired against
a big sun suspended over northwest mining towns.
As I drive, the sky discharges insects like shot
from a sawn-off scatter gun, the windshield
a slaughterman's visor – then, as I crest
a bald rise near the Overlander roadhouse,
the magnified face of James Dickey
looming through a squall of warm Korean rain,
one eye closed for greater accuracy,
the other open though glazed over with communist
blood and flaksmoke. How such visions manifest
themselves is a cruel mystery – no more
disturbing image have I entertained, especially
when considering the extensive necrology
of Australian road travel. I tried to anticipate
Dickey's response to the carnage: would he
pause to comment sadly on the lines
of kangaroos lying stiff-limbed like exhausted
travellers under brown coats on the verge,
or would his approval be rapturous and long-
winded over such a display – ripe potential
for working poetry from the death of animals?
He offered no response, preferring to maintain
a low and tight-lipped altitude. So I hit
the coast road trying to shake him, and found
Kalbarri calm with pensioners taking the sun,
melting long slivers of ice from their bones.
I got out for air and found the poet unhitching
his face from the dusty trailer of my wake.
Before I could speak, he entered the water
and went out past the lines of breakers,
his great ruddy head going under like Easter
Island stone. I saw him offering directions

to a stalled cavalcade of rainbow-scaled reef dwellers
wafting south on the Leeuwin current,
bearing aloft like seaweed the tattered remains
of a child who'd gone overboard off Exmouth
during the light-tackle gamefish tournament.
Her parents were still sending up orange flares
from the dunes and combing the shorebreak
for her clothes, for anything that would provide
some proof of her existence in the world.
Dickey offered the child his blessing, his tears
licked away by an attendance of small blue eels.
When he climbed from the foam he recited
"The Performance" haltingly through a mouthful
of shells and sand, as if trying to make
some connection between his headless friend
and the child whose death he'd only just mourned.
The shadow of a touring cloud fell upon him
and he was gone, his face and voice entering
my eyes and moving there like great poetry.
Then I was driving again, and as if to ease
the burden of such a wild and troublesome
possession, a scattering of Port Lincoln parrots
wearing collars of black feathers came loudly
over the road – spears of green light shrieking
away into the trees. I drove, and the sky let
down its colours. And somewhere outside Cataby,
something like a Tasmanian Tiger was tearing
at itself, doubled over in saltbush at the roadside.
I expected James Dickey to reappear, to kneel
beside the animal and question it on the nature
of pain and extinction. But nothing emerged
from the cloud of dust and flies the creature
was writhing under, its muscled flanks veined
blackly with tyre burns. And then a blowout
doing ninety, almost hammered to scrap metal
by a wheat truck, the driver's finger out the window
carving *fuck you* in the air –
torn rubber melting over the handle of the jack,

my spit fizzing like eggwhite on hot gravel
beside the flattened body of a bobtail lizard,
its blue tongue rolled out thick with jumping ants.
Outside Yanchep, wildflowers lit the spaces
between gums locking into each other, making
a twisted canopy, though some were bleached
and falling, rattled with dieback, flushed
with salt, or whatever it is the root systems
of the west have been drinking from earth
infected by grubs, mismanagement or chemicals.
Fourteen hours from Carnarvon to Perth,
the huge Capricorn skies diminishing the further
south you drive. No music. No talk. The surreal
attentions of an American poet and the legacy
of his company: a passenger seat ablaze
with purple flowers – pickings from a walk
through fields of Paterson's Curse – the bees
in my hair, droning like Dickey's farewell
reminder: *Be sure to utilize the skin, bones*
and organs of everything you see, and remember,
no landscape, no outcome is predictable.
I stop at a Swan Valley vineyard and throw back
tumblers of claret at a tasting. I buy three
bottles, open one, and slug dry vintage
recklessly as I go, market gardens becoming
the outer suburbs, the late sun caught redly
in a tilted bottleneck. Half pissed by the time
I roar into Fremantle, a few surfers paddling in dusklight,
the poetry of a long drive on the make,
the engine killed, and the last bottle
drained off like communion in a carpark
overlooking the sea.

The Mercenary Heart

An American poet, walking on a farm outside
Carson City, Nevada, found blue feathers
and bones caught in fence wire.

Perhaps it was because she knew her native birds
so well, or because what she found inflamed
a need to record her own fragmented life.

Whatever the reasons, she reconstructed
the death of a great blue heron
from the moment it left the nest to the time

the wind chained it thrashing to the barbs.
For my part, I'm indifferent to the bird's death –
to what happened between its low flying

through Nevada farms, its arrival at the wire,
and how it looked when the poet
chanced upon its remains. What really gets me

is that I can read her poem, take what I need,
then write something worth preserving of my own,
completely ignorant of America's native birds

and the poets that use them, alive or dead,
for inspiration. I've seen the bristling
crucifixions of eagles on Australian farms –

feathers, talons, and straw-thin bones
stitched against the wind like a cruse
that rarely fulfils its black intentions.

And I've considered, in passing them,
using their flightless warnings to fire
the poetry I promised myself I'd write one day –

words like bones, gathered and assembled
into the myths their various functions
have invented out of air. My reasons

for writing this are difficult to explain,
that is if there are any reasons at all.
Though, as with the American poet

(Blue Heron Death as therapy, a theme
lifted from the wire), the warnings have gone
unheeded, and the poem has made it through,

knowing any action can be used
and justified when the mercenary heart
has been out hunting once again.

Tidal Dreaming

You wake and tell me that your dream was tidal –
the rattle of stones, the miles of salty wind
giving voice to trees and honeycombed caves.
You tell me quietly about the gentle rocking
motion of the waves, your warm body moving
slowly upon my body, advancing and receding.
And as I listen I remember that I too
had been dreaming, that possibly I had taken
leave of my body's sleeping anchorage.
In the wide bays of each other's arms
or sleeping alone, our places in the bed
still wear the positions we made as we turned,
seeking comfort or space in the dark.
No need to question how far we travel
when, behind our eyes, time and distance
disengage their symbols to flicker and collapse
like glass in the skylight of a kaleidoscope.
When I lean forward to kiss you, pine needles
fall from my hair. On my skin, a smear
of charcoal where fitfully I'd passed,
brushing burnt-out trees. And it seems
you were there beside me, flying over
the wreckage of week-old fires – in your hair
also, the evidence of pines, on your skin
the ash-grey stains.   Coming to rest,
we gathered ourselves into wakefulness, moving
again with moon-drawn water, our voices
returning from caves and forests. And silenced
by morning's pale-blue noise, our shadows
passed with belief in love beyond the tired
streets of light and work, our heartbeats
measured by the pulse of the waves, incoming
deep and regular. To sleep beside you
is to know the secret dark each other's
dreaming has encountered – forests and caves,
where stalagmites and stalactites
grow towards each other like patient tongues.

from
COLD WIRES OF RAIN

Cold Wires of Rain

On the sun deck of the *Sealink*,
anchored to a blacktailed wind,
three storeys over Holyhead's
smoking houses and fishing boats
beached at an angle by the run-out tide,
I am belted to the rail by cold wires of rain.
Watered-down blood
drips from the wires of my guitar:
a fingertip peeled to the nail
while strumming a border ballad.
As the engines turn over
like a giant with a chest infection,
I play to a small attendance of drinking men,
the heads on their pints blistered with rain.
Seagulls lift off
to hang themselves like torn flags over the stern.
The men pitch their glasses at the waves.
I wipe blood from the finger board,
turn from the rail,
and step over puddles of vomit
like a three-dimensional field-guide
to the front bar of The Spaniard at last drinks.

Half an hour from Holyhead,
and already there are gaping holes
in the sides of duty-free cartons of booze,
stacked like sea chests on trolleys and seats.
An empty can of Heineken clatters into the bar
where I stand, staring down at my pint;
it's an aerial photograph
of a white-capped, inland sea.

Four pints later, on the sun deck again,
reading a selection of Patrick Kavanagh into the wind,
a voice from the dark asks for "Raglan Road".
I play it, with congealing blood
like brown sap streaking the wood grains.
A woman moves into floodlit rain to sing:

a voice that could be rising
from the throat of Nina Simone.
The song ended, through a veil of tears,
she tells me how her lover
parked his car on the shore of Lake Ontario
and walked out naked, in the snow, to his death.
Under the windscreen wipers,
an envelope glazed with ice:
Protect thyself from the world, it is hunting thee.
She looks down through her hair
as if into the news of death.

On the sun deck, alone,
the lights of Wicklow flickering to starboard, I stand
at the rail of a boat on the Irish Sea
and confront the knowledge
that I am constantly leaving –
a man obsessed
with whatever seems important at the time:
gulls and passing drunks,
black water folding into itself
three storeys below ...
      The voices of strangers fall
to line the pockets of air each departure makes.
Now, it's the memory
of the smell of a grieving woman
that has me timing my heartbeat with an opened finger
in the cold, in the driving rain.

from
THE VIEWFINDER

Rats

There are rats in the compost.
                                        The compost contains
the spores of Legionnaire's Disease.
Each morning
              an easterly wind brings the sound
of rats hacking their thimble-sized lungs out.

I watered the compost yesterday.
              Five rats surfaced
                              through rotting melons
and egg shells. Their bones seemed to vibrate
under sleek grey hair
                    as they coughed
                                  and flecked
the shells with their blood.
            I've started coughing too.
                    Last night I cracked a rib.

When I went out to the compost just now, the rats
were silent,
            curled inside a gutted melon.
When I coughed they stirred, and one of them
looked at me.
                It was shaking uncontrollably.
I carried the melon down to the beach, and buried it
in a ghost crab's hole
                      a dog had recently excavated.
            Then I sat back and coughed,
                  and waited for the tide to rise.

from
SKINNED BY LIGHT

Strategies for Confronting Fear

On a day without wind, it takes fifteen seconds
for a telegraph wire to stop vibrating

once a currawong has vacated it.
I've timed the wire in the wake of sparrows, finches,

but their body weight, being equivalent to twists
of air-borne weed, disturbs the wire

as would a brief visitation
of cloud and its fine, concomitant rain.

The heart rate of a fieldmouse
under the dropping shadow of an owl

would be easier to read
and less demanding on the critical faculties.

In a blue squall of rain, a raven alights on the wire
and uses its tail like a counter-weight

as it balances, shits and balances.
On a train station platform, a woman

in a dress lit with shapes of flowers
is also watching the raven.

A train arrives, then departs like a strip of film,
her upturned face in a frame

as it passes over projected light.
When I look up, the raven has gone, the wire still.

I estimate its vibrations would have lasted
fifteen seconds, but I am conservative and scared,

preferring averages to the day's
complex arraignment of statistics and potential lies.

And although I have an imagination,
it surfaces rarely, in thought and word:

the sharp black flight of a raven from the wire,
a woman watching it go ...

I wanted to call out to her, to challenge
the cold bright air and the way she moved into it.

I would have said: "Let us praise
the luminous scar on the perineum.

Let us curse the indignity of revival, and summon
strategies for confronting the names of our fear!"

But instead, as sparrows blow down
like bits of bark from the wire,

as a woman is travelling, I wait, tense and silent,
for a chance to record

how imagination can make durable, singular,
fragments from the most common of scenes.

Reversals

THE RAIN

The rain loves it
when, at night,
in bed, before sleep,
it listens to the sound
of sheets of tin
falling on its roof.

JOHN O'HEHIR

Orange clay and stones
pour out of a hole in the ground.
A coffin follows them
like an abstract elevator
that won't open, and is lifted
from the hole by six men
who, walking backwards,
seem unconcerned
about the difficult terrain.
They slide the coffin
into a black sedan, which follows
a line of cars, their headlights on.
The coffin is opened
in a back room that could be
a set from *Days of Our Lives*,
where a man in a black suit
removes makeup from the face
of another, black-suited man.
Blue-lipped and cold,
the man is carried to a car
and driven to a white-tiled room,
where vital organs are placed
into his body. He is then taken
upstairs and put to bed.
Over his head, the green static
line on a cardiograph screen

with its accompanying
high-pitched whine, stutters
and becomes a steady,
sidelong graph of jagged edges.
The man opens his eyes.
On a trolley, he is sobbing quietly.
In the back of an ambulance,
his wife is praying and holding
his hands. At home, she puts
the telephone receiver down.
In the bedroom, the man gets up
from the floor and clutches
at his chest. A few minutes later,
in front of a mirror, sweating
heavily, John O'Hehir
is conducting Bizet with a chopstick.

The Coral Trout

The Coral Trout is unrecognisable as it flies
out of the toilet and enters his mouth.
A deadly parasite the trout inherited from
a coral reef inflames his intestine.
He replaces the trout's eye and swallows
a laugh. He lays flesh like pearled moss
over its bones. Standing on the deck of a boat,
he forces a hook into the trout's mouth,
then lowers it into the sea. This process takes
time and patience. Finally, the fishing line
whips back and respools itself onto the reel.
He seems amazed to find another,
smaller fish attached to the end of the line.
He removes it and spits a mouthful of beer
into a can.

Rural Myth

Inside a fire-gutted river gum,
in Victorian high country,
large corrugations of bones.

Devout attendants of putrefaction:
beetles, worms
and blowflies, their eyes

the colour of spleenblood,
leave the flesh to match itself
to a fallen frame.

When the animal stands,
unsteadily, it walks away,
its melanistic spots

matching perfectly the fire-
blistered bark of the gums.
Some days later, at a road,

as if it had been
trained for this, a panther
leaps backwards

into a cage that has opened
after a circus truck
failed to negotiate a bend.

The Red Kangaroo

The red kangaroo rises up
in a field of saffron thistles, and throws
four greyhounds from its body.
A whistle, which means *kill*,
enters a young stockman's mouth
like a threadworm.
The dogs return, thistles
clicking into place behind them.

Thanatos

Come to any lookout in the mountains.
    Approach the edge as you would
        a weeping friend whose back is turned.
    Grip the finger-polished rail.
Look down. It's best if the view
    unfolds through a gauze of mist
        or cloud: the shapes of gums,
    the silent explosions of tree-
ferns in a blue dissolve.
    Look down. Your feet are those
        of a stranger – someone standing
    on the edge of their life, surrounded
by the prints of other lives.
    If there are wet leaves
        on your shoes or skin;
    if a small ant has stalled
at your heel; consider these as gifts
    and return your gaze to the mist,
        to fragments of ferns and trees.
    How often have you been high enough
to step away and die? The pipeline
    over the suburban creek
        when you were young, stranded
    on cold metal between two fans
of spikes, the insides of your thighs
    going numb, currawongs swooping
        from stringybarks, calling
    continue, continue,
when all you want to do is turn back,
    but you're frozen there, inching forward
        over rusted steel and fear.
    Or halfway up a waterfall,
your fingers testing smooth green rock,
    feet splayed out, soaked to the guts,
        swallowing thoughts of death
    as tiny friends throw stones
and reckless encouragement
    from where they stand beside a foaming pool.

             Dropping from a pipeline
        or high wet wall when you
are young, you rarely die.
             You are taken from the air by a silent
                  arrangement of wings
             and placed into bed,
your underarms and thighs a puzzle
             of bruises the colour of week-old bandaids.
                  Step or fall away when you have
             lived long enough to dismiss
the sound of a guardian angel's wings
             as wind through lofty leaves
                  or waterspray, and you'll break
             open, spreading over creekstones
like dispersing, clotted silt, your bones
             the sticks you once floated as boats
                  the length of a careless day.
             So what rises or falls
inside you now? Do you sail feet or head-
             first into a fog-buried canopy
                  of trees, or do you walk away,
             only vaguely troubled
by what captured you there
             by a cold, singing rail, the breast-
                  feathers of a crimson rosella
             smearing your face, mist
in your teeth, swaying at a barrier?
             Imagine yourself in a free-fall
                  to certain death.
             Does imagination die before
the body? The prayer or scream
             you let fly on the way down
                  will be silenced
             by the head's incomprehension.
Before you turn away, say your name
             and count the seconds it takes
                  for the name to be repeated
             from rockface or the face

of someone else who has come
 to stand between the need
  to live and the need to fall.

Skinned by Light
Get your compass and your sharpest knife ...
                               John Gorka

Wind shear over mountain grass
does not spook the feeding animal,
yet its legs collapse at the end
of the length of a wind-sounding arrow.

A shadow falls where blood is pooling,
and a man's face, mirrored
poorly in a dead buck's eye,
changes shape as the night comes on.

The man will write of this;
he will turn Southern State acreage
into animal heaven, fenced with nylon
strings strained to open tuning

by six post-riding swamp birds,
bright as machine heads.
From two wars and fifty game seasons,
winged then grounded, with blood

in the yellow crosswires of his eyes,
he worked earth and air
for the trace elements of desire:
on platforms nailed high

into deciduous light; on the gun-
metal blue skin of rivers
printed with trout rings and a poised
oar blade, in the spoorless myth

of the last Arkansas timberwolf ...
He knew the position of the gland
that releases the hormone of death,
and he tapped his plated skull

as if testing the density
of a blighted sugar-melon; as if
taunting some well-established,
word-addled ghost of the head.

He could read, in the tapering
kinesiology of flayed water
moccasins, the concentric,
height-defining circles on a map

of the Blue Ridge Mountains,
and then he'd go, into the trees
and sky for days, laying traps
for language in unlikely places:

in a clearing after a murder of crows
had abandoned their whirling dervish;
in balled prisms of nettle water;
under pines where the wolverine

bleeds its thread of pheromones.
And once, beside a river,
watching the surface-mouthings
of a steelhead, he sat without moving

until the fish had turned to words,
then he stood, cleared a difficult
syntax of finned reeds and bubbles
from his mouth, and fired

one last invective at the deep
image work of his contemporaries.
When death came at him
from downwind of a hospital bed,

it did not wear bright plumage,
scales or fur. When the shadow-lines
of trees passed over him, they did not
seem the skeletons of animals,

as he would have made them,
in some other time, on a sleepless
night watch over deskwood.
But when sunset skinned the wall

of the ward, there appeared, between
bed posts propped like a pair
of cast iron fire dogs, flamelight
from a stone-bordered hearth

in Carolina, and he saw himself
lying down in wet clothes, cold
and steaming, drained of poetry
at the end of another season.

from
THE SLEEP OF A LEARNING MAN

Aurora Australis

The Aurora Australis enters the river
like the corner section and three floors
of a burnt sienna building come adrift.

Its decks are a mobile installation of gadgetry.
Apart from bunks, it's one big laboratory.
It has returned from the south, having been

where horizons are defined by a skua's wing,
where a shout can carry a thousand miles
through the signal stations of home-

sickness and breaking ice.
Its log-book records krill and weather,
how solitude works on the hemispheres of the brain.

It comes in, tugged and twinned on a city tide –
a serious boat with a crew that could be
people lounging at any dockside railing:

polar-necked and capped, not visibly brilliant
at any trade involving migratory ice or wind
– they talk quietly, economically, they stare

and do not startle when, approaching land,
a bull seal bellows
twice, and overlong, from the bridge.

The Rain

Rain, and driving thoughts of rain, miles
and hours of it, inches and yards of light
and dark rain, where seamless cloud has been
stitched and gathered into a great undoing
of itself, in wind that brings its freeplaying ride
through a highland plateau down into the hair-
pinned, run-off green below Mount Arrowsmith
or Frenchman's Cap, whose faces have gone
to a full-blown curtain of angled rain
and its bright companions, ice and snow,
to make, under the button grass, a blackwater
seepage from a thaw that will come within days,
or less, here and there at rain-mined overhangs
flowering with spillage, and in Queenstown,
where a conveyor belt sounds like a mongrel
dragging its chain against the rim of an over-
turned drum, it is raining still, at the tail-end
of a mining era, on the open-cut towns of Linda
and Gormanston, diminishing under seasons
of rain-blurred windows and the shells of cars
in yards overgrown with absence, on lakes
where the rings of rising trout are one
with the surface-pelting blanket of the rain,
clear and clean as the spittle of a local,
weather-telling prophet who grinds lens glass
and peers at the sky from a roof, rain-hammered
and domed above streets awash with longing,
and further afield, near a moored house boat
on Macquarie Harbour, an old woodcutter
is remembering rain as an all-night, fly-sheet-
testing wall of black proportions, and day
as much the same, with sunlight no more
than a rumour, with running silver on the chip-
flecked sleeves of his oilskin, and now, inland,
with no change to the long-range forecast,
at Cemetery Creek and Laughing Jack Lagoon,
it is raining, and the rivers are full, their black
mirrors bubbling, and even the mountain-fed

torrent between two hydro-electric plants
– its peaks and lines like whitewashed milestones
tumbling end over end – is driving the blood-
made turbines with its own internal rain.

The Sleep of a Learning Man

When I woke my body
    was idling, my teeth vibrating.
There was much to consider
    lying there in the dark
beside my son, who was
    sleeping with his legs
tucked under his chest
    as he did in the daguerreo-
type images we saw
    of someone doing a knee-tuck
under a shifting film
    of blood grains.
Too late for sleep, I tried
    to imagine other positions
a scanned and floating boy
    might assume, and why
I was humming to my bones
    in bed. I turned over
to the right shoulder, lifted
    my head, and looked into it.
I saw a puzzle of coils.
    I heard a valve pump
labouring to clear
    its body-feeding lines.
Whatever my son said then
    as he breathed and moved
into another position
    and name for sleep
held words of comfort,
    and I found myself
drifting from thoughts
    of a troubled heart
into what his first sentence
    would sound like, what

it might contain, and when
    it would surface, there
on the open border
    of his second language –
words with the ability
    to calm himself and the fitful
sleep of a learning man.

In Late September the Dunes

In late September the dunes
stop moving, as if a seasonal migration had ground
to a contoured, abrasive end.
Marsupials keep to low stands of trees

where they remain
shy of each other's breathing, and feed
on a hard, downwind spiral of listening.
Nights have been flawed

without possums coughing over
the water tank, and walks are barren
with no flashlight
twinned in the eyes of a potoroo.

No one, driving, slows to give themselves
safe passage past a sand-blow.
The only danger, now the dunes have stopped,
is what imagination does

with pockets of roadside shadow, at speed,
and the peripheral after-burn of a little raven
hopping to a road kill,
as if wallaby bones made music, as if

more than a vehicle's wake
were blowing through its leg feathers.
In late September the dunes
shut down, and what has taken shallow root

– feather, footprint, rainfall, stone –
will flourish until wind erases them, beginning
again a ribbed advancement
of sand and curious animals.

New Poems

Fruit

Edible stamen, slow emergence
of under growth
and over-grown erectile tissue ants investigate.

Fleshed and riveted fruit of hermetic climates,
by your grounded, opaque skylights
may you be known;

by your sweet hexagrams
like portals into tapering sleeves of risen flesh
may you be eaten.

Take this wealth of succulent season
into the heated, unrepentant language of your mouth
until it is compliant and involved,

until the tongue withdraws
spiked with splinters so tiny
they could be the breaking windows of saliva bubbles,

when all that can be said, in parting,
in breaking down, has been said
and turned back into the earth.

Spring Equinox

Having heard her speak, and then mime a description
of how she intends to balance a brown, still warm,
free-range egg on its tapering end, I practise alone
with a white, thin-shelled egg some battery hen

had abandoned to its tray on a row of death.
All attempts to have it stand are met
with the muted, rolling sound of shell on polished wood
and then silence before the crack and flow

of yolk so pale, you can almost see and smell
the horomone-injected gruel that shaped it.
And now she is ready. She has no degree from the School
of Ancient Wisdom. She has not professed

to having found a way to tame the laws
of gravity or its sisters Air and Breaking Ground.
She tells me it is only now, in the equally-weighted light
and dark of the Spring Equinox, that an egg

can achieve its own equilibrium
under cover of a wind-governed season where, like an obelisk
seen from a distance, it will appear to have been
upended and planted for good, unknown reasons.

Before she begins, her instructions are clear:
no music or heated discussion, no movement near
the blackwood table she has chosen, and as for the hen
responsible for this fine, tactile specimen, she can

maintain her vigil, one-eyed and flicking through
the cartoon frames her head makes at the window.
She leans in and over the egg as though warming it
with her breath and the long dark panels

of her insulating hair. Her fingertips make a cage,
allowing the egg enough room to move until
movement diminishes and then stops, and when
her hands rise and angle away, as if two spiders

in the cool, remarkable joinery of their skins
had been startled from copying each other,
the egg demands and receives my attention.
I inspect it, as close as my breathing

and loose clothing will allow. She joins me,
saying at dusk the egg will topple, cold and out
of kilter with the spell-binding work of the world.
With the mountain drained of perspective and light,

the egg falls down, and rocks to settle on the wood.
When I hold it, something wrought from pure
amazement forms, dissolves, then reforms
in the quartering chambers of my heart.

The Wandering Albatross

It's as though the Continental Shelf
with its east-facing rifts and cliffs were visible;
as though the full-bodied waves that blow over it,
freighted with kelp, tidewood
and the bloated bodies of dead seals
were thermals, sideways tracking
and printed with spirals
that mark a slow convergence
of warm and nutrient-rich, cold water.

What rides this marriage of elements
does so with a wingspan
hammered from great distances,
its feathers containing worn emblems
and fading lines, such as might be found
within the pages of a passport
from a time when travel was slow,
when destinations involved a leaving
of smoke and waterlines
while crossing the world's oceans.

Breeding and exhaustion
are this wanderer's only reasons,
in all weathers and seasons, for flight.
Coming in from the South, it angles away
and down, almost wetting the tip of its leeward wing
before raking a dimpled currentline
for upwellings of cuttlefish, chrome-
plated splinters of schooling sauri,
or a sampling from its own reflection,
which it swallows, saltwater being
an elixir for this long-range survivor.
And when, after days of gliding,
its hollow bones take on the ache
of being all at sea, it will follow a ship,
inspecting it for mast wires,
an unpeopled railing, for anything
upon which to perch.

To find a mate, the females gather
on barren outcrops
surrounded by suitors, each one
expectant and competitive
in the sleek, wind-tailored plumage of their kind.
Having found each other, they remain
at the centre of the cycles
of company and separation
for up to eighty years,
despite long absences, despite their differences.

See them coming in –
white gliders with landing gear
that paddles for purchase
on the stones of sub-antarctic islands
where their mates are waiting, alike
and yet unique, their singular scents and calls
dividing a raucous field with welcome.
One partner. One life, together.
And for every egg that grows
and breaks under terrible weather,
a fledgling will emerge
to test its wings and stand its ground
for nine months, and then leave
to circle the globe, solitary
in its preparations for love,
the sensory avatars of sea and air
made manifest in the compass glass of its eyes.

Fly Agaric
for Lisa Gorton

In a forest I found what I'd not been looking for
and yet, having found it, I began dissecting
    fact from speculation
        until my findings had been reduced
to a basketful of speckled caps
the colour and texture of the skin
    of woodland creatures
        that would rather bleed
themselves into shallow plantings in the earth
than succumb to capture.
    When I had gathered enough
        to darken a baking tray
and fill the preserving jar my son had used
as a window through which to view
    the cycles of the lives
        of water-beetles, I began the procedure.
With a *Field Guide to Mushrooms*
laid open like a journal for everything you need
    to know of the natural and the medicinal,
        I separated stems from spore-
concealing gills, then peeled the skin
from caps whose shapes ranged from circles
    torn and buckled to those resembling noses
        long-discarded by their owners –
these I opened, making cross-sections
for internal observation, having found them to be
    deeply scored with cyst-
        like markings, as if some
dermatologist-come-pointillist had been hard at work
to clarify, repeatedly, the meniscoidal flowers
    and blood-seeding,
        fibrous roots of melanomas.
With the oven set and timed at two hundred degrees
and half an hour, the door ajar to release a rising damp
    of sweat, thus assisting dehydration,
        I prepared a dram from thistle of milk
as a liquid counter-measure to nausea, knowing how

hallucinogens announce themselves in the lining
of the gut then spread from there,
       in all directions, ending
in a concentrated re-configuration of the head.
Dried, they seemed benign, as when, in death,
     the electric sheen on the skin
          of a reef-dwelling fish dies out
to become the colour of what remains
when coral's living organisms starve, flushed
     from their cells by algal blooms.
          Having chosen Bulgarian mouth-
music to begin and complete what I'd planned,
I drank an elixir distilled from an essence of weeds.
     As for the caps, I left them
          to further reduce in the oven
until they were black, until the mouth-music
had drained from the speakers, as if I were hearing
     an end to the wild,
          muscaria-heightened dreams
of exhausted Berserkers. In truth, I was a fool
to look for visions, knowing they exist already
in the eyes and harvesting hands.
     I went out next morning to walk again
          in the spore-leaving dark,
and I read from the dense mycology a forest
floor reveals, though now, beyond all thoughts of narcotics,
     I turned back and saw how the light
          was dispersing, needled and combed
into shifting spools that unravelled on nothing
but random thrivings of pretty toadstools.

Lighthouse

Beneath the oldest and southernmost lighthouse in Australia,
I look out to where Petra Branca, the last outpost of land
before Antarctica, seems ready to pull anchor and drift away.
I can no longer measure distance in miles, or the number
of hours in the months since you left – the frequency
by which thoughts of you arrive as quiet interruptions
to each day, like a pain in the chest that soothes as much
as it alarms; the way an intimate moment can lose perspective,
as if the emulsion on the only photograph I have of you
has been worn away by neglect or reckless handling –
these are the markers that tell how far I have travelled.
I could wait for carpet rolls of mirrored light to be thrown out,
to contrast and compare the flourish and sweep
of their regulated warnings with the clarity and confusion
of hoping to find you where you do not wish to be found,
but I've seen enough. I will leave before dusklight
blows in with bronchial flowerings of spray from the swell
that breaks on the headland's cobbled, club foot,
before daylight trades its wide-angle lens for what happens
in the dark room, and I'll look for you again
where the landscape advances and recedes, where trees
and sky make the radiating lines of veins that make
a supernova at the base of your spine, or that place
behind your hair, just below your ear, where my lips
and breath never failed to light the blue touchpaper
of your desire.

Live Sheep Trade

A generalised, accepted assumption of stupidity
rides in five storeys of steerage.
Loading begins at birth, and ends with lesions
and bruises wool conceals.
    A stick across the face
           means nothing when pain
is registered by the rolling of eyes
and a few perfunctory shakes of the head:
a lump like the makings of a third horn
on the head of the sheep
who required assistance while boarding.
An equator crossed is a line of heat
that turns the metal rails of pens
into stripped electrical wiring,
unearthed and designed to hold,
at standing-room-only temperature,
ten thousand cross-bred shanks, necks, loins
and legs, all destined for the killing floor
of a halal table.
    For *Shy Feeding Syndrome*
           read death by starvation.
For *Scabby Mouth*, read beltings, the sickness
of motion and dehydration.
The sun is a windlass the crew use
for lowering and applying heat treatment
to the internal organs of every animal
deserving of special attention.
A cruise ship is at its most beautiful at night.

Hurricane House

In the Capricorn tropics, in the season
when sunrise lights its hurricane lanterns
and dusk settles down to watch over them,
a land-bound, monitored wind arrived
to lift the sky's stained glass mantle
and blow the lanterns out.
This was when Tina, or Karen, or some other
system of raw, feminine weather
had been upgraded from unstable to extreme.

In town, storm windows had been fastened,
potential projectiles removed from yards,
and while most understood
that survival is equal parts preparation
and remaining calm, there were always those
who went out to watch the horizon seethe,
the ocean incandesce like lit alcohol.
Some stayed on at the outer limits of their alarm
until the sky came apart, or down, and then they ran,
outlined as negative images of themselves
in frames cropped by fork lighting.
One man, who'd known cyclones to strip the coast
to its bones, watched these outsiders
develop from a dark solution
of heavily-timbered rain, until they were gone
from sight or from their lives.
In the waterside room of his simple living
he made a shelter from tables and there,
by torchlight, he opened
  Meteorology For Beginners –
    not that he was in need
      of rudimentary information
but because he wanted to say the names
of cloud formations out loud, to read again
of how weather balloons work, and what the tropo-
sphere can tell us about ourselves.
In the morning he climbed from a wet
quilting of splinters and palm fronds

into the rinsed, unlikely brilliance
of a break in the storm
and he looked up, small with knowledge,
as he'd done at the height of the night's undoing,
the pages of the weather book scattering
like the wings of hand-fed birds
and he was, once again, laid open
with expectation, more alive
than he could remember, with the need to learn.

What the Executioner Means

It's not only that I haven't slept for something fast approaching
thirty hours, or that the humid Berlin afternoon, darkening

under a unified fall in ambient light and barometric pressure
has intensified the senses, especially touch and smell

so that fountain water, approached and palmed absent-mindedly,
returns like memory to the nerves in the hands, reminding them

of just how good a thunderstorm can be, when it breaks,
not the rain exactly, more the atmosphere, the cool flush of air,

the ions, negative and vaguely influential, and how,
in her passing and stopping to lean her bicycle against a wall,

a woman leaves the scent she had applied to her neck or wrist
that morning, one that's been changed by the slow,

confidential workings of her skin, so that what I inhale
could be rose geranium, smoke and coffee, and although

these things will leave me, they will not leave me alone,
for whatever's been causing this unease, this sense of being

at odds with a city and its weather, it seems it all began
somewhere over the Middle East, at thirty eight thousand

cloudless feet, pinned to a window seat by a widow
from Sweden, who believed she had found in me a captive

sounding board for wistfulness and grief, yes, it began there,
with the illusion of being stationary at a groundspeed

of five hundred miles an hour, and as she spoke I looked away
and down to find the lights of a major harbour,

its golden lines laid out with such precision and intensity,
they could have been the body of a steel guitar or electric,

oversized oud, and still she continued, even though my responses
to her late husband's infidelities had gone from mono-

syllabic sympathy to silence, she went on, her voice becoming one
with a General Electric drone, though soon after we'd passed

the lit harbour, she stopped talking and went to sleep,
her small hands veined and ringless in the reading light,

and turning back to the window, I found we were over
the Gulf of Persia, where twin flames were leaking

from an oil rig or burning tanker, so high, their reflections
were advancing and receding with clarity, giving substance

to blacked-out water, and I remembered the interview I'd heard
before leaving home, I was lying down with the radio on,

troubled by some minor conflict between reason and the heart,
and I heard an executioner from Saudi Arabia talk

of how the spilling of blood is God's work, how his wife
and children help to clean the sword after each killing

and how, when he turns the blade over in his hands, at night,
he can see two fires burnishing the metal, and he broke down then,

saying, breathlessly, *I understand them, I understand them*,
and from where I lay in bed, from where I sat speeding

over the earth and Gulf, and from where I am now, sleepless
 yet alive
with expectation, having just returned from the Garden of Exiles

where I left two stones as memorials to the family of a friend,
it comes to me, as three Turkish men play the day to a close

acoustically, it comes to me, I have no desire to be troubled
by what the executioner means.

The Grave of the Southpaw

Those who claim to have found it
can offer no direction
or tell you what was written on its stone,
if there is one.
      It lies beyond cartography,
           beyond the oral shape-
shifting of local history.
By the wind-and-moon-drawn animations
of bracken shadow
that is always broad and speculative
as any sighting,
      the grave of the southpaw
           continues to be passed over,
underfoot and undermined by our
refusal to accept small miracles
without some kind of proof,
      be it physical, or fleshed
           in at least eight megapixels.
The son of the son of the painter
and docker who went three rounds
with one of Jimmy Sharman's finest;
the man whose job it was
      to nail full black moons
           to the highest points of a shire ...
Had someone asked them,
before they went to earth or flame,
they may have told of the grave's location
and why so many have tried
to find it with their lives.
In the Daintree Forest, after
the dawn chorus, a cassowary draws a line
through leaf rot and fig slime
then steps back, lowering her helmet
in a gesture of acceptance or defiance.
And now the grave is visible.
      It grows from the lie
           of the land, in photography
that is aerial and angled widely

over hard terrain. It grows from where
a flock of long-billed corellas
have been harvesting,
despite the timed reports
of gas guns, and the more distressing sound
of a farmer tearing his hair out
in what had been a wheat field.
      Who will tell of this?
           Who will acknowledge mystery
and its spark of deep recognition
when it comes to them?
When the grave of the ambidextrous one
reveals itself, in the high country
of our need to believe,
in the hinterlands of our having all
but given up of being
    arrested by amazement,
some will understand and be
overwhelmed before moving on,
while others will riddle themselves
again, and then again,
with the details of what might have been,
or of what is yet to come,
and they will remain,
    with their compass
        and their sharpest knife,
trying to hear the faint register
of a heartbeat of imagination.

Four am, Nuclear Medicine

Negotiating silence in the hospital chapel,
a nightwatchman alternates
between lifestyle magazines
and another incomplete meditation
on his own mortality.
In the Deep Image room,
the mapping of some-one's heart is still evident
in the afterglow of rays of cathode
screened as capillaries
and the blocked-in walls of arteries:
a spotlit waratah in the clinical dark,
a four-chambered sequencing
of blood-flow under stress.
Someone wheezed on a treadmill here
as a doctor eyed the heart-rate monitor,
then needled the blowing walker
with an isotopic dye.
In Nuclear Medicine, the floor
is panelled with fine shadows,
as if the day's ECG printouts
had been left to feed over scuffed linoleum.
Results divide and multiply
into news both hard and celebratory.
A cough dies out on a wall
in the only carpeted room
between diagnosis and chaplaincy.
In the following silence, a troubled heart
can be seen as a difficult flowering,
as the after hours art of science and medicine,
but I prefer the all-terrain-
and-weather mongrel attitude
of one rider, with no fresh horse
and nowhere to go but home.

Scarves

A headscarf can mean discretion, old-style religion
without song and dance, a cover
for pinned and rollered hair protection, or hair loss
during a poisoncure course of medication,
when scarves, worn by women in public,
signal an approach to the end of their living,
or a life in the balance, in question, in remission.
A scarf in wood is one step towards the down-
fall of a tree: the bright, open angle of the cut
defining where the trunk and whistling crown
will lean, then track an undergrown litter of shadows
to settle in a brief disturbance of birdcalls
and displaced wind.
    A scarf can be style and warmth,
        though trimmed to its essence,
like the word kerchief, and fastened with knots
at the edges, it becomes Southern European
dialect for building site fashion.
I once saw a satin bowerbird wear a scarf
on the back of its prospecting head
as it rearranged all things blue in its place
of seduction – though it might have been the pockets
of bleached summer grass I was looking through,
lying as I was in a state somewhere
between the personal and the pastoral.
Perhaps there was no bird at all,
and the need for gathering bright material
had befallen me, not altogether unexpectedly, again,
and I returned to a word or gesture
like an animated cry of timber or cancer,
and I waited for something to happen,
for no other reason
than my love of expectation, and now for this.

Luge

They slide away
like bodies at a sea burial:
free-divers who failed to rise in stages,
    fallen aerialists
        for whom the safety net turned
to a grid of hard shadows on the earth.

Sleeved in a tight, second skin of colours
they have willed themselves here
    to a cutting
        frozen waves have made from the swell,
their long trajectories
breaking seconds into fractions,
as if their passing had been
reduced to statistics, as if they still needed time.

Gathering speed, they pass
oceanflowers of shaved ice
    and the gleaming squama
        from what might have been
flying fish, or skin
shed from where a winding sheet had come loose.

On a sliding scale of weather and memorial,
they are numbered and set free
in all their identities,
when the stop-bath of a water clock
    thaws and dovetails
        its cogs and wheels,
releasing them from where they lie
helmeted and bound in Nordic fashion.

Coming to rest, they sit up
as the dead have been known to do,
    as if surprised
        at finding themselves no longer horizontal
under a faint sifting of applause or snow.
Leaving, their names light the scars
and hollows that show where they have been,
having made it to the end
of this life, and in record time.

Biographical note

ANTHONY LAWRENCE was born in 1957 in Tamworth, New South Wales and is one of Australia's most highly-regarded poets. He is the author of twelve books of poems, the most recent being *The Sleep of a Learning Man* (Giramondo Publishing, 2004). His books and individual poems have won many of Australia's most prestigious awards, including the Judith Wright Calanthe Award (Queensland Premier's Poetry Prize), the Harri Jones Memorial Award and the Gwen Harwood Memorial Prize. He is also the recipient of a Senior Fellowship from the Australia Council – one of the most prestigious funding awards a writer can be accorded in Australia.

His first novel, *In The Half Light*, was published by Picador (in Australia and in the UK) in 2000.

Anthony Lawrence lives in Hobart, Tasmania, with his son Cormac.

Also available in the
ARC PUBLICATIONS
International Poets series

LOUIS ARMAND (Australia)
Inexorable Weather

DAVID BAKER (USA)
Treatise on Touch

DON COLES (Canada)
Someone has Stayed in Stockholm

SARAH DAY (Australia)
New & Selected Poems

GAIL DENDY (South Africa)
Painting the Bamboo Tree

ROBERT GRAY (Australia)
Lineations

MICHAEL S. HARPER (USA)
Selected Poems

SASKIA HAMILTON (USA)
Canal

ALAMGIR HASHMI (Pakistan)
The Ramazan Libation

DENNIS HASKELL (Australia)
Samuel Johnson in Marrickville

DINAH HAWKEN (New Zealand)
Small Stories of Devotion

BRIAN HENRY (USA)
Astronaut
Graft

RICHARD HOWARD (USA)
Trappings

T. R. HUMMER (USA)
Bluegrass Wasteland

ANDREW JOHNSTON (New Zealand)
The Open Window

JOHN KINSELLA (Australia)
America – A Poem
Lightning Tree
The Silo:
A PASTORAL SYMPHONY
The Undertow:
NEW & SELECTED POEMS
Landbridge:
ANTHOLOGY OF CONTEMPORARY AUSTRALIAN POETRY
ED. JOHN KINSELLA

THOMAS LUX (USA)
The Street of Clocks

J.D. McCLATCHY (USA)
Division of Spoils

TRACY RYAN (Australia)
Hothouse

MARY JO SALTER (USA)
A Kiss in Space

ANDREW SANT (Australia)
The Unmapped Page

ELIZABETH SMITHER (New Zealand)
A Question of Gravity

C.K. STEAD (New Zealand)
Straw into Gold
The Right Thing
Dog

ANDREW TAYLOR (Australia)
The Stone Threshold

JOHN TRANTER (Australia)
The Floor of Heaven